STARV

WHEN LIVERPOOL

RULED THE SKIES

STARWAYS:
WHEN LIVERPOOL RULED THE SKIES

By

Patsy Leigh

BRAMBLEWOOD
PUBLISHING

Bramblewood Publishing
3, Bramblewood Close
Overton-on-Dee, North Wales, LL13 0HJ

Email: Bramblewoodpublishing@outlook.com
Website: www.bramblewoodpublishing.com

First published by Bramblewood Publishing, 2016

ISBN: 978-0-9954996-0-7

Designed and typeset in 12pt Palatino Linotype by Robert J Davies
Printed and bound in Great Britain

Photograph of sky with vapour trails used on front cover reproduced under licence from Shutterstock, © Graeme Dawes
Cover design by Robert J Davies

ABOUT THE AUTHOR:

Patsy Leigh was an Air Hostess for Liverpool's Starways airline from 1960 to 1964. Patricia Collins, as she was then, was born in 1934 in Wormley, Hertfordshire, and grew up during the Second World War. Her father died in 1943 and her mother, aged 27, was left with four children and a rented house which they had to leave. Patsy attended eleven schools from five years old until one month before her 14th birthday, after which her

Patsy with grandson Rupert

mother needed her to work. Patsy worked in Garners, a London restaurant, for almost seven years, before training with Revlon as a manicurist and beautician, working at hairdresser Henry da Costa's salon, Number 9, New Bond Street, and next door to a very young and broke Vidal Sassoon. After that she moved to Norton's in Duke Street, St James, where her clients included actors Sir Alec Guinness, Trevor Howard and Leo Genn, and the Queen's surgeon.

It was in part due to Patsy's brother-in-law Laird Kennedy, himself a pilot, that she first took to the skies. 'He thought I would make a good stewardess,' she says. Now, aged 82, Patsy looks back fondly at four years spent up in the clouds with Liverpool's very own airline.

This book is for:

My late husband, Captain George Keith Leigh

My two wonderful sons:
Dr Robert Leigh and Dr Christopher Leigh

Our amazing grandchildren:
Kimberley Leigh
Abigail Leigh
Hugo Charles Leigh
Giles Henry Leigh
Rupert Edward Leigh

And the people of Liverpool for four of the happiest years
of my life.

ACKNOWLEDGMENTS:
I would like to thank Robert Davies, an author in his own
right, who gave his precious time to help and encourage me to
put this into print.

Patsy Leigh

~~~

The publishers wish to thank Trinity Mirror, proprietors of
the Liverpool Post & Echo, for kindly giving permission to
reproduce the photograph overleaf, and those on pages 106,
137 and on the final page.

Air Traffic Control at Liverpool Airport, Speke
Photograph courtesy of the Liverpool Post & Echo

CONTENTS

INTRODUCTION

DOWN MEMORY LANE

LIKE an enormous Chinese lantern the full moon hung over the darkness of the airport, its wintry glow casting shadows over the deserted landscape; a magnificent stream of light seeming to stretch like a river into eternity.

A great feeling of warmth spread through me as I reflected on the old days. But should I have come back?

Earlier, I had lingered outside the main terminal building of Liverpool's Speke Airport. It looked derelict. The boarded up and broken windows and the entrance drives were overrun with weeds, debris, nettles and litter where once there had been manicured lawns. I stood there totally speechless, feeling an anger which melted into sadness.

How could they? Whoever they were, who let this happen to such a lovely old building? In 1960 this had been the gateway from Liverpool to the world, so busy, vibrant and alive. Thousands of passengers had passed through its doors daily on their way to far-flung destinations.

I could almost see them now: the coachloads, the private cars, the taxis, the luggage, the children, the milling, thronging crowds that had invaded this building almost twenty-four hours a day. Now all was empty and silent apart from the heavy traffic that sped by on the main road.

Later, I returned in the darkness and walked slowly towards the wrought iron railings which surrounded the airfield – I felt the cold as they almost stuck to my gloveless hands. How often I had walked – walked!? – most of the time almost running and out of breath past these railings. The bus had stopped at this corner and we would walk – or run – the last quarter of a mile, ever fearful of being a moment late, overnight bag in one hand and shoulder bag in the other.

Warm tears involuntarily trickled down my cheeks, clouding the vision of a now shimmering moon. In 1960 we had set off from here and travelled the world but had always returned to Liverpool with an overwhelming feeling of warmth and belonging.

I could not begin to count the times we had taken off and landed from this now ghostly-looking runway. I pressed my forehead against the hardness of the iron railing until it hurt.

Sadly I didn't have the sense (or maybe the time) to keep a diary of those extraordinary years. Yet suddenly, from misty, tearful eyes, I could see the silver underbelly of a Dakota, its top painted white and one blue word 'Starways' on the fuselage; circle of stars on its tail – its wing almost clipping the railings as it slowly taxied past.

Turning, and with its engines at full power, it

lifted into the night. Before I could gather my thoughts, the four engines of a long-range Skymaster, the moon dancing on its four propellers and large silver fuselage, taxied into view, turned and roared after the Dakota into the darkness. My eyes were playing tricks, I turned my gaze to the road, glad to see the familiar sight of my car. What I had just seen wasn't there.

Last Flight By Dakota

Dakota aircraft, which have been used by Starways on the Liverpool-London night, to-day finished their service and will be replaced by the four-engined Viscount. Pictured above on the apron of Liverpool Airport, as passengers board, is the last Dakota to leave for London this morning.

Article in the Liverpool Echo marking the Dakota's last flight with Starways

I got into my car feeling secure in its warmth and comfort and the present returned. I wanted to turn on the ignition and go – back to reality, but my hands wouldn't move. I just sat motionless wanting to go – yet wanting to remember.

Above all, wanting to let people know how proud this airport was; how important and loved this once-beautiful listed building was to so many.

I had returned for this trip down memory lane

several years after Starways and the old Liverpool Airport had been consigned to history, I was not to know then how, much later, it would thrive again as a wonderful hotel complex and that the airport itself would be reborn as Liverpool John Lennon Airport.

But that day, amid the weeds and debris, I wanted to remember what Starways and the old airport meant to the city of Liverpool and its people in its 1960s heyday. And I knew that I had to tell my story and not let this wonderful past die.

CHAPTER ONE

MY NEW JOB

HEATHROW'S only passenger lounge was suddenly silenced as the Tannoy sprung to life emitting unintelligible words through its loud-speakers. Then, after a pause for breath – the muffled words were repeated.

I watched the people, their ears straining to hear something that sounded vaguely familiar, begin-ning to look confused and bewildered as the sounds died away. That spring day in 1960 was my very first time in an airport departure lounge. I had sat alone in a corner, eyes firmly fixed on a small check-in desk that had the word 'Starways' in big bold letters above the counter.

The Station Manageress had instructed me not to go far from sight so I had remained in this same seat for well over an hour, totally unaware of the time that had passed.

Sunrays filtering through a small skylight settled on my face and warmed my head. I watched, fascinated, as the multitude of passengers came and went from many directions. I had never realised how entertaining people could be. My thoughts were interrupted as once again the public address system sprung to life but this time the voice was crystal clear, each word separated by a pause and with unbelievable definition the voice almost sang: 'Starways – announce – the – departure – of – their – Dakota – flight – to – Exeter – Newquay – and – Liverpool – Will all passengers proceed to Gate Number One.'

My heart gave a leap. At the age of 25, this was the flight I was to take to my new job. It seemed a whole world away from London and so, with a heart beating too fast for comfort and a mixture of thoughts – of apprehension on leaving London and excitement of travelling to the unknown – I joined the slow-moving crocodile of passengers to Gate Number One. As we passed the check-in desk, the owner of the voice smiled at me as she lifted the microphone to begin her second announcement.

She was attractive, a sort of Dorothy Lamour with thick, dark hair crowning large, dark eyes. She gave me a wink of recognition as she began to speak but oh, that voice. I had to turn away and stifle a grin. The crocodile, now outside was making its way towards the Dakota across the tarmac. We slowly moved onto the aircraft steps and then we were inside.

After the bright sunshine the aircraft appeared very dark and as we entered I saw nothing but a lone stewardess nodding a welcome to each passenger. Then, seated in the last back seat on the left-hand side, I watched her in awe as she calmly and confidently went about her job of settling passengers for take-off. My eyes remained glued to her every move. This could be me someday I thought (if all went well).

Yet somehow I couldn't quite picture myself doing this and as the door closed to the outside world I felt a sort of sinking panic. My thoughts were interrupted as a distinguished-looking man took the seat next to mine. He turned towards me and smiled as he began to fasten his seatbelt.

I watched him and did the same. 'I believe you are joining us.' He looked at me and smiled, 'welcome.' I took his outstretched hand. 'Captain Dunsmore, Patricia Collins,' I said.

During this time I hadn't noticed that the aircraft had slowly begun taxiing. Now it turned onto the runway. As the Dakota's engines were opened up to full power the noise completely drowned out any sounds within the cabin. It bumped along the vast Heathrow runway for what seemed like forever and then I held my breath as I felt her lift into the air like a giant bird.

The sun gleamed on the window as I looked out into what was an endless blue and felt an over-whelming sense of freedom and elation. And though during the next four years I would lose count of the number of take-offs I'd experience, the thrill of this first time would never quite leave me.

But for now, all the cares of the world seemed to have been left behind and the unknown stretched endlessly ahead somewhere in this blue eternity of exciting experience. During the flight, my eyes became firmly fixed on the busy figure of the air hostess. This could be me in the 'not too distant' future, a wonderful dream that sent my imagination into overdrive.

CHAPTER TWO

THE ADVENTURE BEGINS

LANDING at Exeter and walking into the passenger lounge, which was then little more than a large Nissan hut, brought me sharply back to reality. The passengers who were now waiting to go on to Newquay in Cornwall sat around on hard wooden benches looking at almost bare walls.

The place held little charm and even less enticing was the bleak picture from the terminus windows, as a rolling fog began to move across the greyness of the airport like a giant Swiss roll blanketing out our view completely as it engulfed the building. In a state of excited euphoria I started to experience my first long airport delay.

Minutes ticked by and turned into hours as we waited for encouraging news from the Control Tower but the fog remained thick and unmoving with passengers and crew settled into this isolated world. Suddenly, the Captain appeared and addressed the passengers.

He left no-one in doubt that if we were to reach Liverpool that night we would need a miracle and his final words were that his First Officer would answer any questions we may have while he was off to sort out hotel accommodation.

The First Officer introduced himself as Frank Carroll. His looks were those of a Hollywood star and his sense of humour was apparent from the moment he opened his mouth. After all the questions were answered Frank still stood there in the centre of the floor, head on one side enquiring 'can anyone sing?' The silence that followed his question was absolute.

'Dance, then?'

Undeterred, Frank grinned warmly at the faces surrounding him, a few relaxed and smiled back but no-one made a move.

'Right,' he said. He then bent down and began to roll up each trouser leg to his knees. From the back of the room I watched in amazement as he captivated his audience with a star performance of 'When it's cherry blossom time in Stratton, New Jersey, we'll have a peach of a time.'

The Captain, who had returned during this performance was now giving a tolerant, fatherly shake of his head as the passengers began enthusiastic applause and the smiles were wide and unanimous. As the applause died away the Captain, suppressing a smile, raised his hands for silence. 'Ladies and Gentlemen – Ladies and Gentlemen', he repeated, 'I'm afraid this flight crew is now out of duty hours and we will be spending tonight in Exeter.'

Sitting over in one corner of this vast room I found it hard to believe that such a short journey to Liverpool had become so much of an adventure –

shortly afterwards we were all clambering onto a coach to go to our hotel for the night.

After an unsettled night we all returned to the airport for what seemed like a dawn take-off. I was to learn later that the aircraft was required back in Liverpool before 9.30am. So after an uneventful flight, I was beginning to take things in my stride as we touched down smoothly onto the runway of Speke Airport.

Starways G-APEZ Douglas DC-4 Dakota with Pratt & Whitney Engines; speed 240mph; 78 seats. It was 'everybody's favourite aircraft,' says Patsy Leigh.

In the middle of Speke Airport's lounge I stood, even more bewildered as masses of humanity pushed their way back and forth through the terminal building and I tried to find the Starways check-in desk.

'Miss Collins?' I turned to see an attractive girl in

uniform coming towards me. I took her outstretched hand as she introduced herself as Betty
Gillian (which I knew to be the name of Starways'
Chief Stewardess), 'you should have been here last
night.'

She paused, looked at her watch and continued:
'I've no time to talk now – look, collect your
luggage, see Mr Kent (she pointed to a slim sandy-
haired man who was besieged by bodies) and ask
him if you can leave your case behind the reception
desk. I'm about to do an Ostend flight – aah –
maybe you had better come along.'

She continued to talk as she began to move. I
nodded and walked beside her. 'You should have
been on another training flight, but with the delay
last night perhaps it's better if you come along with
me.'

The horror of the Ostend trip could never be
glamorised. The weather was horrendous and the
aircraft seemed to do everything short of actually
turning upside down. I vomited for most of the
flight and the look of disdain on Betty's face only
served to make me feel worse.

Miserable, and near to tears at Ostend, I followed
limply behind the crew as, laughing and joking,
they made their way to the airport restaurant. I sank
into a chair feeling like a wrung-out dishcloth, yet
so relieved and thankful just to feel firm ground
beneath my feet.

Our meal had been pre-ordered and I felt nausea
rising in me as the starter – a large tomato filled

with prawns and mayonnaise, was placed in front of us. The crew cleaned their plates in moments, making way for the enormous steaks which followed, topped with parsley butter, and surrounded by fried potatoes, French beans and mushrooms.

One pilot cut into his large (very rare) steak. My arms remained rooted to my sides but the crew appeared unaware as they ploughed into their meal. They are not human, I thought, as another wave of nausea engulfed me followed by the horrifying awareness that I had to board the aircraft again for our return flight to Liverpool.

Death seemed dearer to my heart at that moment. However, not only did I survive the return journey, gradually feeling a whole lot better, but the month's training that followed was fantastic, and so I became a Starways hostie. I would learn that Starways was better known to the aircrew as 'Fred Karno's Outfit' and that I would become overworked on the lowest possible pay but that any source of slander from outside our airline would be met by a reaction of fierce loyalty which can only exist between the overworked and underpaid which we were to a man.

So as my first weekend with Starways disappeared like a dream, I was on the return flight to London and it was make your mind up time. Should I collect the rest of my worldly possessions and emigrate? Having never been north of Watford until now, my family thought it a step in the wrong direction. But I had tasted warmth, friendship and a loving, deeply human Liverpool. The Liverpool people to me had seemed to belong to a vast, interconnecting family. I had felt something special from the moment I set foot on Speke airport, almost fatefully my mind seemed made up for me.

Patsy with her brother Michael in RAF uniform at their mum's house

CHAPTER THREE

TALE OF THE MISSING SHOE

ALL this, of course, didn't stop me shedding quite a few tears as I boarded a train to take me north to Lime Street Station. One week later on the long journey I thought only of family, friends and London. At Lime Street Station the amount of luggage I had brought with me meant the necessity of taking a taxi to Speke airport.

And there I stood once again in front of the still-busy traffic office, invisible among passengers eagerly waiting to check in. Bewildered, I stood among those crowds wondering where I was going to live. Starways had accommodated me for one night in a Garston hotel. But the next day the onus was on me to find somewhere to live.

Suddenly, someone noticed me left behind like a piece of luggage from the disappearing crowd. Someone offered me a cup of tea. Weary from my travels I explained I was a new member of staff and need temporary accommodation until I could find something permanent.

One girl took pity on me and suggested an aunt of hers who lived nearby on the Speke Estate. So, with a slip of paper in one hand and just one suitcase in the other, I set out to find the house.

Finally I approached the door, its gleaming brass knocker a huge pixie sitting on a toadstool. Taking it in my hand, I was about to let the heavy weight drop when the door opened and I practically fell on top of a smiling, homely-looking woman.

'Mrs Fisher?' I stared into her friendly eyes, 'I've been sent' – the sentence was stopped in midstream as I received an all-embracing bear hug. 'Oh come in, love, and call me Auntie,' she exclaimed, grabbing my suitcase in one hand and taking hold of my arm in the other. She smiled and hugged me again, 'let's have a cup of tea, love.' I followed her into the kitchen not realising my heart had been given, there and then, to the City of Liverpool.

'Auntie' was mother to all, her vocation was to

look after all who crossed her threshold. She had one son with learning difficulties, a simple soul who, like his mum, loved everyone. The house was a nest of warmth and love.

The first month of training with Starways consisted of almost non-stop flying, eating and

The photo of Patsy which her mum always kept safe in her purse.

sleeping. There was no time for homesickness, no time even to think, as I was exhausted. The month passed in a flash and there I was, standing before Betty and being told 'tomorrow you go solo'- a Dakota flight to Rome. I felt a dream had come true.

The following morning I arrived well before the crew in a brand-new uniform and full of Auntie's breakfast. I could hardly contain my excitement, everything seemed unreal as I carried out the duties I'd been taught the past month.

My memory of that outward journey to Jersey, Lyon and Rome remains blurred. For more than seven hours I busied myself doing anything and everything for the passengers and by the time we arrived in Rome a reassuring smile had permanently fixed itself onto my face. And I felt pleased with my performance.

My flight was Starways' first Rome flight of the 1960 season and although we had a full load of passengers on the way out we were scheduled to return empty. In Rome the next morning we arrived at Champino Airport for our passengerless non-stop return to Liverpool. The Captain, James Tickle, and First Officer Frank Carroll, went off to file a flight plan. I waited for their return in the airport lounge. Jim returned much quicker than expected, telex in hand. He said we had a change of plan and were positioning to Dublin.

Soon after this we departed Rome for Dublin with only tea, coffee and biscuits for sustenance. Needless to say, when we arrived at The Royal

Hibernian, our Dublin hotel, we were famished. Not having eaten since breakfast, we didn't shower or change but made our uniformed way to the hotel restaurant. As we sank into our seats around a large table, I realised that my feet, clad in new shoes, were killing me so the relief of kicking them off under the table was heavenly.

We ate and ate as only aircrew can. During the meal our Captain informed us we would be taking Dublin passengers to Lourdes early next morning. 'So', he said finally, 'I'd like you to retire as soon as possible and get a good night's sleep.' Jim then rose from his chair and so did Frank and I – with one shoe on and the other foot desperately foraging for its mate.

'Well, let's go,' the Captain spoke again. I bent and looked under the table only to find a bare carpet. 'Excuse me, Sir,' I said almost in a whisper, 'I can't find my shoe.' Jim looked up from signing the bill with disbelief on his face. Then they both stared at me before diving under the table muttering, 'shoe, shoe where are you?'

I stood, pink with embarrassment, as the heads of our fellow customers turned in our direction. I waited until they appeared from under the table-cloth and their puzzled looks told me they had not found my shoe. By now all the guests and the waiters were looking in our direction.

'Are you sure you had it on when you came in?' said Captain Tickle. 'Of course, Jim, I wouldn't have been able to walk with only one high heel on.' Near to tears and tired, I sat down as they began their search again. I began to wish I was anywhere but the Royal Hibernian and how could I take off for Lourdes at 6am the next morning minus one shoe?

I pictured myself delaying our flight and possibly losing this wonderful new job. Both pilots' heads appeared once more from under the table, sank back into their chairs – with empty hands spread in despair. Now very near to tears I felt completely bewildered.

Suddenly Frank (our First Officer) snapped his fingers at a waiter and said: 'have you seen Madam's shoes?' 'Shoes, Sir?' 'Shoe, one shoe,' replied Frank.

A waiter appeared from behind me, an enormous silver platter in his hand, and proceeded to lift the large bulbous lid slowly in a very theatrical fashion and there, nestled amongst dark old leaves of lettuce was my shoe. I had had my first lesson in how to acquire a sense of humour. I felt upset and cross but laughed with relief at seeing my shoe and saving my job.

Our flight to Lourdes took on marathon proportions and it was one week later that we were to return to Liverpool, having completed Liverpool-Rome; Rome-Dublin; Dublin-Lourdes; Lourdes-Rome; Rome-Dublin-Liverpool.

On arrival at Liverpool, Mr Kent (our Traffic Manager), bounded up our aircraft steps, hands open to receive the ship's (aircraft's) papers. 'Collins,' he heaved a sigh as he repeated to me,

'Collins, since you left somebody calling herself Auntie has been bombarding us with telephone calls, saying how dare we send you away for a week with only one pair of knickers! Will you kindly inform Auntie that we don't count hosties' knickers before a trip!'

CHAPTER FOUR

FUN WITH THE AIR CREW

FRANK Carroll, the pilot who had been on my very first Starways flight, had definitely missed his calling. Extremely good looking, thick black hair and eyes as blue as the sea. He also had a great personality, was full of fun, a wicked sense of humour and was everybody's friend – and everyone warmed to Frank.

Our airline captains looked fondly on this First Officer as they would a high-spirited son, but there were two captains that Frank himself had a great rapport with – Captain Don Hammond, who was Yogi Bear to Frank's Boo-Boo and Captain James Tickle who was Stella to Frank's Rita. I might just add that all three were very male and happily-married men.

My first trip with Yogi Bear and Boo-Boo was on a long-range DC4 with another stewardess, Fay Arista. We flew 80 passengers to Rotterdam for the weekend. At the request of the flight crew, we girls each took half a bottle of whisky off at Rotterdam. On arrival at the hotel we passed the bottles over to pilots and arranged to meet them later for dinner.

Rotterdam's hotels were fully booked that weekend so I was sharing a room with Fay, and Don had to share one with Frank. Fay and I relaxed – bathed, had tea and finally decided to phone the men to see what time we were going out to dinner. We rang and rang their room but there was no reply.

We let another hour go by in case they were out, then rang and rang again. 'Bet they are in the bar,' we said almost in unison and so down to the bar we went, but the place was empty. We rang their room again from the reception desk – still no answer. So for a little exercise we decided to walk up the four flights of stairs to room 417.

As we approached the pilot's room we heard a ghastly noise, a cross between a tropical rainstorm and turning-out time on a Saturday night. Reaching the room we found the door was open, every light switched on and the noise was now deafening.

Both Fay and I shouted into the room from the doorway but it was obvious no-one would hear us. We ventured in, still calling. On the right of us the bathroom door was open – the shower was full on, a voice was singing loud enough to open the heavens and there, sitting cross-legged on the floor of the shower was Don in bright blue swim trunks, a towel turban-style around his head, and the shower raining down on him. He held a cigarette in a holder away from the water and was singing at the top of his voice.

On we went to the main room and there stood Frank spread-eagled against a wall, eyes cast towards heaven – he didn't seem to notice we'd arrived. Our eyes then came to rest on a desk where two half-bottles of whisky stood empty. 'How could you?' we chorused to Frank. Dressed for our evening out, we felt cross and now very hungry. 'What are you doing, Frank?' said Fay. 'Sh-sh-sh,' he whispered, 'I'm a tree and I'm growing.'

As we turned to go, Don appeared, two soaking towels around him and one still on his head. 'Girls,' he pointed his now soggy cigarette at us, 'girls, tonight we are going to be millionaires.'

'All we want is something to eat,' said Fay. 'Millionaires,' repeated Don undaunted, 'I know the best restaurant in Rotterdam.' 'Are you fit to go anywhere?' we stuttered. 'We,' continued Don, 'will be fit and ready in half an hour, so down you go and wait in the bar, girls, and we will join you.'

Half an hour later our crew appeared looking remarkably sober and smartly dressed in lounge suits. Outside the hotel we hailed a cab and Don gave the driver an address which turned out to be Rotterdam's most exclusive Indonesian restaurant.

Fay and I were overwhelmed by the vast menu and all agreed to let Don order our meal for us as he had been there before. That done, we relaxed and supped our beers as we awaited our surprise feasts. Soon a gigantic dish of delicious pork satay was put in the centre of our table.

The pork with peanut sauce and a large basket of bread rolls disappeared in minutes. Next, a large half of lobster was placed before each of us and the table was covered with every salad imaginable. We ate and ate until we couldn't move.

'That was great,' we smiled, sat back and lit cigarettes. 'I'd like a coffee,' said Fay. 'You've got to eat your steaks first,' said Don. Steaks!! Three heads turned and stared. 'Steaks,' repeated Don and no sooner were the words out of his mouth, when the largest platters I'd ever seen filled with steaks, onion, tomatoes, mushrooms and a large bowl of chips were placed before each of us. Four portions of asparagus were followed by a large bowl of salad.

Patsy wearing her Starways uniform in Lisbon, 1962

Fay and I sat staring at the food. Unable to eat, we watched the men take mouthfuls. If, of course, we had known that our entire weekend's food money had gone on this one meal we would certainly have asked for a doggy bag or two.

But we never forgot that weekend with Yogi Bear and Boo-Boo. The exclusive restaurant, the elaborate meal and our stomachs full to bursting on that Friday night, and how hungry we became on Saturday and Sunday. Because apart from the hotel's continental breakfast, which was one bread roll and jam, not another morsel passed our lips until our return flight. Don never mentioned the word 'millionaire' again, not even jokingly.

Jimmy and Frank (alias Stella and Rita) were known as 'The Rome Kids' simply because they seemed to fly more to Rome than anyone else. The Starways Dakota would graunch along via Jersey then Lyon (for fuel and food), arriving in Rome after seven or eight hours of flying. Added to this were our stopping times and 'reporting for duty times' so we were nearly always on our flight limitation of 16 hours by the time we reached Rome.

As I reported for what was to be a four-day trip, I was awash with excitement. This would be my first real chance to see the Eternal City, having only had exhaustive night-stops until then. The weather between Liverpool and Jersey was foul, the seatbelt sign remained ON all the way and more than half the passengers were sick.

So, unable to take my seat, I spent the time com-forting and reassuring the passengers. It was a great relief to open the cabin door at Jersey and breathe in fresh air after the smell of stale vomit. And I spent the next half hour cleaning the cabin for the next leg of our trip.

The weather settled for the journey between Jersey and Lyon so we opened the Bonded Bar and began to serve tea, coffee, juice and biscuits to those who wanted them. As we approached Lyon we announced how long the aircraft would be on the ground for our much-awaited welcoming meal, and a chance to wash and brush up. But soon after landing we had to make another announcement as, apart from Air Traffic Control, everyone else was on strike.

The French ground staff handling our aircraft had done their best and gathered together 36 makeshift sandwich packs for the passengers. The flight crew were not so lucky as the goodies did not stretch to crew so we would all, again, enjoy milk and biscuits which I took to the pilots an hour into our flight.

Frank smiled as he took both mugs of tea from me and, turning to Jim, said, 'Stella, I suppose these hosties have their uses but we have four days in Rome, I wish we were alone.' Jim gave me a sideways wink and grinned at me. Shaking his head and turning to Frank he said, 'when you've finished your refreshment, Rita, could you manage to do some information slips for the passengers?' I grinned and left them to it.

We arrived in Rome well over our 16-hour duty limit to find half the city, including our hotel, blacked out by a power cut. There had been a massive storm as we had landed and we arrived wet, tired and very hungry, also in need of a bath and change.

Needless to say, the pilots made straight for the bar. I followed behind and was overjoyed to see a bar festooned with dishes of nuts, crisps, olives, anchovies etc, and we were hungry. Two large tankards of beer were placed before the men and were half empty before I decided (not being an alcohol drinker at that time) that a glass of sweet wine might be good. The wine turned out to be a tumbler full and tasted so good I drank it down in one go.

'Right,' said Captain Tickle, 'let's get out of these monkey suits and go and find a meal somewhere.'

As I got off the bar stool my head began to go round and gingerly I made my way to the lift – putting one foot in front of the other had become quite a problem. All three of us got into the lift and gratefully I leaned my back against its side for support.

As we began to ascend my back slid slowly to the floor and I ended up in a sitting position. The pilots took an arm each helping me out of the lift to the door of my room. 'Thank you both,' I muttered. 'Are you all right?' said Jim. 'I'm fine,' I smiled reassuringly. I cannot remember taking my uniform off or going to bed but I awoke 12 hours later feeling ravenous, not having eaten for approximately 35 hours.

The boys were already at the breakfast table when I arrived in the dining room the next morning. And while I ate almost everything on the buffet breakfast table they announced that we were all going sightseeing and our very first stop would be the Coliseum. In the historic magnificence of our first stop I was overwhelmed by the splendour and the tragedy of what had once been. We three walked and chatted and I found myself going on ahead eager to explore what lay through each and every archway.

As the pilots had seen all this many times before, they walked slowly, chatting and enjoying the warmth of the sun. Eventually I turned round to say something and found they had both disappeared from sight. So I stopped and waited for them to come into view.

The moments turned to minutes and they were nowhere to be seen. I suddenly felt lost and tentatively began to retrace my steps calling 'Frank! Jimmy!' until I finally reached the point where we had started. Feeling very alone I wondered if they were looking for me. I didn't know what to do or which way to go when suddenly a party of American tourists came into view.

My eyes searched their group for a sight of my crew and as they passed, out of sheer loneliness, I tagged on behind. The leader of the party had been to Italy many times and was commentating on its history as the party chatted about the USA, almost ignoring this wonderland of architectural antiquity.

We moved on snakelike through archways and tunnels. Suddenly my eyes rested on two enormous slabs of stone either side of an archway. Unable to believe my eyes, I saw on one, the kneeling figure of Jim, his head bowed almost tragically into his hands and on the other the standing figure of Frank, his face hidden by a raised motionless arm.

The Americans continued walking and talking completely oblivious. Almost holding my breath I waited until they had moved out of sight. 'What are you doing – oh how could you?' I whispered. They didn't stir a muscle, not one movement from these living statues. 'Please come down,' I began to beg. 'Get lost,' was their whispered reply. Then an American woman spoke from behind me and said, 'Gee! Isn't that just cute.' Oh God, I thought, and went to hide.

That evening at dinner, Frank said to Jim, 'we'll take her to the Via Veneto for coffee, sit outside Doney's and look at the Plaza. The Roman girls are just gorgeous.'

It was a wonderfully warm evening; the city sky seemed host to a million stars as we strolled to Doney's. Outside, we sat and drank our coffee and the pilots had liqueurs.

I sat between the two of them listening to: 'oh, get a load of that one – cor, look at that.' This went on for over half an hour and I was decidedly miffed at the lack of any kind of conversation. So, pushing back my chair a little behind the men, I began flashing a beaming smile at every male that passed, then I lifted my skirt to my knees and looked into each and every male's eyes.

The Italians receiving my attentive smile soon responded. Heads began to turn and some actually walked backwards looking at me. Frank and Jimmy now turned to me and as they did my face went completely blank until they looked away, when again I would beam and make eyes at the next approaching Italian male. Finally, Frank bent across to Jim and said, 'Stella, have you got the feeling something's gone wrong?' I grinned, sipping my coffee as we all began to talk and enjoy our evening.

Not long after this I was with Captain Johnny Soccet and Frank taking an empty aircraft up to Glasgow to position for a flight. A boring one-and-a-half hours lay ahead as I had nothing to do. Ten minutes after take-off I went to the flight deck with hot tea. While they drank I remained looking out into the endless blue of a good flying day.

The Captain motioned to Frank that he was off down the back to the loo. I remained where I was until Frank said, 'would you like to sit in the old man's seat? Go on, take the weight off your feet.' Delighted, I sat for the first time in a cockpit seat and Frank spent the next few minutes explaining the maze of aircraft instruments to me.

'That's what we call the Horizon,' he said, pointing to one, 'see that moving line? Well you have to keep that on the horizontal line and that keeps the aircraft in the correct position.' He then bent over to my seat shouting above the roar of the Dakota's engines, 'would you like to get the feel of flying?'

'Oh, yes please.' I was ecstatic with excitement. 'Right, grab hold of the stick.' I did as I was told and began to feel the sensation of flying. It was marvellous.

Excited, yet apprehensive, I watched the Horizon and held the aircraft steady. 'How am I doing?' I shouted, my eyes never leaving this one instrument. 'Fine, fine, but of course, George is flying her at this moment.' 'George?' I queried. 'The automatic pilot,' he smiled. 'Oh,' I said, slightly disappointed. 'Of course if you really want to get the feel of flying I could disengage George for a while,' and with a grin he did just that, giving me a smile and the thumbs up sign – 'she's all yours.'

Delighted, my eyes never left the Horizon. I was really flying and it felt absolutely wonderful. For the next five minutes neither of us spoke – until I saw Frank getting out of his seat. 'He patted me on the shoulder saying, 'you're doing a great job – keep it up.' Then he started to move away from the cockpit. Not daring to take my eyes off the Horizon I screamed, 'Frank, where are you going?' 'Won't be long,' he gave my shoulder a reassuring squeeze, 'got to make a call.'

I was now too terrified even to turn my head for fear my eyes would lose the Horizon. I could feel perspiration covering the palms of my hands and little beads of sweat beginning to trickle down from my hairline onto my face. Rigid, I sat there for what seemed an eternity, but was, in fact, about 90 seconds.

'Had enough?' There they both stood, calm and smiling. Still rigid with fear I didn't answer.

Frank got back into his seat and Johnny helped me out of his. 'You are really, really rotten,' I said, near to tears as I made my way back into the cabin, vowing never to fall for that trick again.

Returning from an eight-hour flight one day we were met by Mr Kent (Traffic Manager), who informed us that we were to take the evening Liverpool – London – Liverpool route. The crew scheduled to do the flight had been called out on a charter. Our Captain was Barney Potts and he, Frank and I were very hungry. 'First, something hot to eat,' said Barney and we made our way to the staff canteen, better known as the 'greasy spoon.'

'Lunch is finished and we haven't much left,' said the tired woman behind the counter, 'and no eggs,' she added. 'I've got bacon and I've got chips, and I can let you have toast and tea.' Our three heads nodded to let her know that would be fine.

Our hot meal duly arrived and we tucked in, then halfway through and with our mouths full of food, Frank rose from his chair and stood behind Barney. 'I'm now going to give you a quick benediction,' he said, looking pious and solemn, making the sign of the cross over Barney's head.

Frank smiled a wicked smile as he did this. Barney's face turned a pale shade of grey as he spat, chokingly, the contents of his mouth back onto the plate. It was Friday, Barney was a Catholic (so were Frank and I come to that). But poor Barney was devout and not another morsel touched his lips.

CHAPTER FIVE

THE GIRLS

BETTY

BETTY, our Chief Stewardess, was perfect in her job – controlled, firm and appearing unemotional yet always offering a ready smile for the passengers. To us mere mortals Betty's smile seemed to be on her lips but not in her eyes. She watched us work and work she did herself – a conscientious workaholic.

She enjoyed the privilege of doing her job properly and seeing that every one of us did the same. If you did your best Betty respected you, if you didn't, your days could be numbered. Betty also never appeared to be one degree under and never expected any of us to be ill.

So most of us in the beginning were terrified of doing a trip with her but, once airborne, we were always too busy to worry. We just looked on in amazement at the end of any trip as, with not a hair out of place and make-up as fresh as when she started, Betty said farewell to our passengers.

In 1960-61 our Airline was not overstaffed with seven hostesses. During the summer months we took on temporary girls for the new package

On the right, Starways' Chief Stewardess "Betty" Gillian, with hostess Doreen Barford.

holiday traffic. Even so, all through the winter our aircraft were utilised 24 hours a day and we did work hard. One memorable trip started on my day off. The phone rang and yes, I broke the golden rule and answered it. It was Betty's voice with just one question, 'are your jabs up to date?' Leaving the phone I scurried around to find my health certificates then very breathlessly returned to say my Cholera was out of date but everything else was fine. 'Right,' Betty interrupted, 'get it done today and report back to me, we want you to go to Hong Kong.' I replaced the silent receiver – not even a 'please' – and it was my day off.

Betty called a second time. 'The aircraft is in London,' she said, 'so you and Paddy Elston will be going there by train this afternoon. Your crew is in the Skyways Hotel and take-off will be tomorrow.'

PADDY

THREE hours later Paddy and I looked out on a foggy Liverpool from the luxury of a taxi as we made our snail's pace way to Lime Street Station. Fog was right down the line, we were told by the cheerful railway staff, but we were lucky, one train – and one train only – would be leaving in half an hour. But we may well have found it quicker to walk as five hours later we had only reached Crewe.

Dawn was breaking as the train huffed and puffed its way to London's Euston Station. From the station we phoned the Skyways Hotel only to find our crew had already left for Heathrow Airport. We took an underground train and made our way to join them.

Our Captain told us on arrival that our aircraft would be empty to Cairo Lloyd International. Another charter company had lost an engine and we were to fly a new engine out, then take their passengers to Hong Kong. We arrived in Cairo to find the passengers were in a hotel, so as it would take a few hours for the ground crew to replace the engine that we had brought out and put the passenger seats back into position, it was decided we should join the passengers in the hotel.

Within five hours we were back at the airport. Paddy and I had failed to sleep during the three hours at the hotel and with the Sunday train journey, Monday flying and with little rest behind us we took off just after midnight on the Monday. Thankfully, our passengers were a most delightful crowd of Chinese seamen. They were cheerful to a man and wonderfully uncomplaining.

By the time we reached Karachi our 24-hour flight crew were out of hours so this is where we parted – they to a hotel then a scheduled flight back to England. Paddy and I were to continue with a replacement crew which turned out to be our General Manager, Captain Leigh, First Officer Kennedy (who also happened to be my brother-in-law) and Engineer, Bernie Mackenzie.

The Starways finances couldn't be stretched to replace stewardesses so on day three, since our departure from Liverpool, 19-year-old Paddy and I carried on. My brother-in-law greeted me at the cabin door with, 'what's wrong with your face, my Pat?' followed by Captain Leigh who looked at us as though we'd just had three days off.

This was Paddy's first long trip and she was truly amazing. She did her share of the work and more. She was a fair-haired, blue-eyed cross between Annie Oakley and Calamity Jane, never without a twinkle in her eyes or a mischievous smile on her face. She always laughed as though someone had told her a risqué joke; she shook from head to toe, making her laughter infectious.

Paddy and I had both felt very tired during the first 24 hours of flying but that passed, bringing a second wind and revival. On Wednesday afternoon we began our approach to Hong Kong.

Paddy and I, now working like robots, began to prepare for landing. The galley, as big as a fair-sized room, had to be secured. Suddenly there was a knock on the galley door and I opened it to see a smiling Chinese face.

He looked at me and I looked back speechless for in the hands of this little man was a large aircraft tray completely covered in £1 notes. 'For you,' he bowed and thrust the tray towards me, 'for you.' Shaking my head I said, 'no, no.' He bowed again and said 'for you' and bowed yet again and as he did our 80 passengers rose from their seats smiling and applauding. So, very tired, I just stood there, my eyes now full of tears.

By now Paddy had joined me and we waited for the applause to subside then I bowed my thanks and explained we were not allowed to take money. But all he would answer was 'for you' and pushed the tray towards us again. 'You work velly hard – we thank.' He bowed and the applause began again. 'What can we do?' I looked helplessly at Paddy and we chorused, 'what the hell!'

Whatever we did we had to do it quickly. So we both bowed as I backed into the galley with the trayful of money and Paddy stayed in the cabin. As

I retreated into the galley. I could see the open cockpit door and with alarm saw Captain Leigh removing his headset, about to vacate his seat.

As I looked I remembered another stewardess had casually remarked that if Captain Leigh ever caught any of us accepting money he would confiscate it for the RAF Benevolent Fund. Had we not been so poorly paid (£6 per week) and over-worked, I'd have agreed with him.

As he left his seat I let out an 'oh God' and in an instant placed the tray of money on our Duty Free trunk and sat on it!

My heart pounded as my head thanked whoever designed our full-skirted princess-line overdresses. There I sat, my skirt almost covering the trunk and definitely covering the money. Captain Leigh came into the galley looking at his watch. 'We'll be landing in 55 minutes, Miss Collins, and I would like a cup of tea.' 'Right Sir.' I shuffled uneasily but remained sitting on the money and thought: where are you Paddy?

Captain Leigh stretched his arms but remained stationary. I knew I couldn't move and my mind seemed to go blank with fear as I felt the hard tray beneath me. With a quizzical look he said, 'are you all right, Miss Collins?' 'Fine Sir, thank you.' I tried to smile but felt sick.

He added: 'I would like that tea before we get to Hong Kong.' As he finished the sentence Paddy returned and I greeted her like a glass of water in the desert. 'Ahh – ahh' came out with a noticeable sigh of relief, 'could you make Captain Leigh a cup of tea?' I widened my eyes as I spoke to Paddy, trying to signal I couldn't get up.

Captain Leigh gave me one more strange look and returned to the cockpit. Then I stood up and showed Paddy where the money was and she burst into uncontrollable laughter. 'Shush, he'll hear,' I whispered but she couldn't stop and continued until tears streamed from her eyes as I stuffed the £1 notes into a sick bag.

'£68 from passengers,' we told the rest of the crew later. To us it was a small fortune. We wanted to share the money with them (excluding Captain Leigh) but they wouldn't hear of it. 'Well, let us treat you all to a meal tonight,' we insisted. Captain Leigh looked even more puzzled when we said 'dinner was on us girls.' How we had the strength to go out and eat that night I'll never know as we had been awake for approximately 90 hours when we finally got to bed.

It really didn't surprise Paddy or me, homeward-bound from Hong Kong, when we were told we were being diverted to Calcutta with engine trouble. Our aircraft, a Skymaster G-APEZ had been bought originally from Cathay Pacific and with no return passengers, we were now carrying spare parts and an engine back to Liverpool. The aircraft was full to capacity with freight for Starways and there we were, stranded in India.

The memory of seeing a place like Calcutta for the first time will never leave me. I had grown up during the War, seen London blitzed night after night, but this – millions of people sleeping in the street, people starving and scavenging in rubbish, children purposely maimed for begging and the endless sea of hands hoping for anything.

I witnessed all this on our bus drive from the airport to the Grand Hotel on Chowringhee Street, a huge mausoleum of a place, the entrance hall displaying jewels, crafts and tiger skins for £90. All under glass – riches in this other world, as were the bejewelled women and turbaned men. My room, the size of a flat, could have housed 40 people.

Sitting there alone in the vast room, with the shutters keeping the heat of the midday sun out and the air-conditioning cooling me, I felt sadness beyond belief. This was a horror world I'd never even dreamed of. I couldn't eat a meal that night and I felt sad and removed from the crew who seemed to be their normal selves. The next morning I strolled out with what little money I had changed into rupees and began to give some to the children.

Within moments I was overwhelmed by a sea of bodies and hands, and feeling trapped to the point of near suffocation I dropped everything and began to push my way out of the crowd. In tears back at the hotel, I got a severe reprimand from the crew and learnt Lesson Number One. We were to spend five days in Calcutta. By the third day I began eating the curry put before me and by the fifth I was so grateful to be going home to a place as beautiful as England that all else paled into insignificance.

But there was the little matter of what to do with the goodies we had bought in Hong Kong. Paddy and I had spent every penny of our Chinese seamen's money. I had bought pearls for my mother; jade and car-coats (short anorak-type jackets never seen before) for my sisters; two Chinese dresses for me and dresses for my young nieces.

Also, we had 200 cigarettes each and a bottle of spirit. We didn't, of course, have any money left to pay duty so a plan had to be devised. Our Engineer, a very kind chap, got wheedled into opening a panel over the coffee and hot water urns and my pearls and jade went in there along with Paddy's goodies. The rest went into our suitcase.

Our first UK port of call was London's Heathrow and that is where we, plus the aircraft, cleared Customs. We didn't have to leave the aircraft for this so after the last Customs officer disembarked, we took off for Liverpool light-hearted and happy.

A feeling that something was wrong only emerged as we taxied to a stop at Liverpool Airport. Customs officers greeted us as we opened the cabin door. Hearts pounding, Paddy and I looked at each other.

They wanted to search the aircraft. Captain Leigh had by now come down to the back of the cabin and noticed our worried faces. He spoke to the Customs officers and said that he wished to make space for another aircraft and they could do their search in the hangar.

As they departed for the hangar, Captain Leigh turned to Paddy and me. 'Now I want the truth,' he stated. 'Have you smuggled anything on this aircraft?' 'Yes, Sir.' 'What? I need to know now!' Near to tears we explained. 'Get off,' he said, 'and wait for me in the traffic office.'

We waited more than two hours not knowing what fate beheld us. Then a call came through to Mr Kent. 'Collins, Elston,' he said, 'Captain Leigh wants to see you both in his office, now.' We left our cases at traffic and walked to the Starways hangar that held all the administration offices.

Positive we were getting our cards we meekly knocked on his door. As we entered he was dictating to his secretary so we stood shuffling from one foot to another.

'Right,' he finally acknowledged us as his secretary left the room. From his desk drawer he produced our ill-gotten gains. 'These, I believe, are yours.' We didn't answer. 'Now if I catch either one of you ever smuggling again on my aircraft it will be instant dismissal. Have you got that?' 'Yes, oh yes,' we chorused, hardly able to contain our relief. 'Thank you very much, Sir.'

'Don't thank me,' he added, 'you had better thank Bernie, he saved your skins while the aircraft was being taxied over here.' So with relief and joy we went and had a highly-sweetened cup of coffee with Bernie. And thanked him many times over.

URSULA

WHEN the time came to leave Auntie's and find my own accommodation, I also had to find someone to share the expenses of a flat. And for the next two-and-a-half years that was Ursula Larson. Was Ursula beautiful? Is a palm tree tropical?

She was *very* beautiful, very glamorous – rich thick dark hair framed a perfect oval face, creamy olive skin housed Technicolor blue eyes. She was stunning, she also had a wonderful figure and a brilliant sense of humour – and a personality that could remove the blues out of any day. Ursula's nickname for me was 'Betty' after our chief hostess, but only when 'you know who' wasn't around.

Our first home was No. 1 Mossley Hill Drive, a house we shared with another hostess, Faith, and her husband. The husband just about tolerated our presence and allowed us to stay under sufferance. So we tried to avoid him as much as possible.

To be fair to Cedric, he had to put up with girls who spent their spare time playing records, washing smalls, entertaining friends and boyfriends at all hours of the day and night and it really was a lot to ask of anyone.

Faith had the patience of a saint and the nature to go with it. She was kindness itself and a dream to live with. If, which happened so rarely, the magic day came when we all had a day off together nobody but nobody in the house was allowed to

A Vickers Viscount, introduced by Starways in February 1961
for flights between Liverpool and Heathrow

answer the phone in case it was the airport. When
the phone did ring, it cost us a fortune as we then
rang friends and boyfriends to find out who had
called us.

Ursula and I did hundreds of normal flights
together that have now faded from memory. It's
only when things go wrong that one remembers.
Starways had acquired two new aircraft. They were
Viscounts with turbo-prop engines and they were
our first pressurised aircraft.

On this particular day Ursula and I were to do
the first flight to Tenerife on a Viscount. Our pilots,
both Australian, Captain Jack Ellis and Flight
Officer John Morton, came with the aircraft. Jack
had the job of training our Starways crews on this
new aircraft.

Although a very competent captain he had little

knowledge of what was required to run a profitable charter company and that the commercial administration and tight schedules had to be adhered to, to keep our company solvent. So with the Starways perfectly-planned (on paper) trip in his briefcase, we set off for London.

Ursula had limped slightly going out to the aircraft at Liverpool and I noticed she did the same in London. 'Something wrong with your foot?' I asked. 'No, it's fine,' came the reply. The passengers embarking at Heathrow were all Jewish and it was unusual to see men with little Yarmulke hats on unless we were flying to Israel. They were a very lively, happy lot and the jokes were plenty.

Not long after take-off Captain Ellis was informed by radio of a complete 24-hour strike at all French airports. First we landed in Jersey for fuel, the passengers – already satisfied after tea, coffee and biscuits – were happy. Ursula's limp seemed worse but she ignored my questioning.

Airborne again, we opened the Duty Free bar, served drinks and chatted to our passengers. Our next scheduled stop was Bordeaux where a hot meal for passengers and crew had been ordered at the airport restaurant. However a call from Captain Ellis told us these plans had changed and we were diverting to Lyon.

With only Air Traffic Controllers working, Lyon airport was like a ghost town. One little man came to assist us and he was here, there, and everywhere. When we tried to order catering we were told that not even hot water was available. With our passengers still in the transit lounge we made our way out to the aircraft. Ursula was now limping very badly and looked decidedly grey. Once in the cabin I insisted on looking at her foot only to find that it was septic.

So before the passengers embarked I bathed and bandaged her foot. During the next leg of our flight Ursula remained seated on a stool as she handed me the passengers' drinks orders. By now these passengers were really hungry so it was with great relief that I made the announcement that our Captain had radioed ahead and at our next landing they would provide us all with a hot meal. After that there were more smiles, chats and drinks and the passengers were happy.

Unfortunately smiles soon faded after landing when we found it was St Somebody's Feast Day and everything, but everything, was closed. We were now desperate with 76 very hungry passengers not to mention the hard-working crew.

After soul-searching pleas, someone said they could give us enough bread, ham and cheese for 35 people. We told them 'ham' was out of the question so they added 40 pieces of fruit. We had no choice but to take what was offered and mercifully they gave us hot coffee and hot water.

During the next leg, one portion of bread, cheese and fruit was shared between every two passengers and we served coffee, tea and drinks non-stop. If the trip had gone as scheduled via Liverpool, we would have reached Tenerife by 11pm. As it was almost 10pm now and our next stop would be between 2am and 3am our hope of getting hot food was looking unlikely to say the least.

My heart went out to the passengers who were now extremely restless. None could sleep, their tummies rumbled and tempers were becoming short. We did our best to soothe them and tried to explain. I kept two fingers crossed behind my back – please God make the next stop a miracle, which was asking rather a lot from God. He must have thought so too, for at 3am we landed to find absolutely nothing available.

It was hard to face the passengers as they got back on board for the last leg of our flight. After take-off we had to tell them the truth and the balloon went up. In situations like this, it is nearly always the women who are hostile. Probably this is nature's way of ensuring children are fed and looked after. We had no children on board, which was a blessing.

During the next hour the situation became almost unbearable. To say the women were annoyed would be an understatement and the men, who up until now had been philosophical, began to grow angry.

To be trapped at 21,000 feet with 76 hungry, unhappy passengers is not a pleasant feeling but we had no escape and only one course of action to try and calm down this mass of angry people. They, of course, had every right to be angry and we felt extremely sorry them. In that situation it is not the easiest of tasks to be cruel and hit people below the belt as I was about to do, but it had to done.

I took two or three deep breaths as my fingers tightened around the microphone and began: 'Ladies and Gentlemen, we cannot,' – I hesitated and took another breath – 'express in words how very, very sorry we are for what has happened. We know how many long hours you have gone without food as we have, also. This has been caused by a succession of unfortunate events which have been completely beyond our control.

'The Captain has done all that is humanly possible to get a hot meal for you or even a cold meal but to no avail. You are all very angry and quite rightly so, but we still have over three hours flying before we reach Tenerife. We still have one tin of biscuits and hot coffee or tea which we will now serve. It may help to forget our hunger pangs if, during the next three hours we could spare some thought for the six million people who lost their lives in concentration camps during the last war – our plight may not seem so bad compared to theirs.'

I put the microphone back into place and pressed my forehead against the aircraft bulkhead. How could I have said that? Fear momentarily overwhelmed me but courage had to be mustered to step inside the cabin.

So Ursula, (still limping) and I, at each end of a trolley, took a deep breath and sallied forth. I don't know what we feared or expected but it certainly wasn't the love and warmth that greeted us as we stepped out into the cabin.

I hardly dared raise my eyes but when I eventually did, they were met by other eyes – most smiling – some with tears. The passengers will never know how much I wanted to put my arms around them all and say sorry, I felt so humble and ashamed. But it had done the trick and the remainder of the flight was delightful. When we landed in Tenerife we had been flying for 18 hours.

BELINDA

WHENEVER a few hostesses were gathered together in the airport bar, they mostly had a moan about our low pay and hard work. We chatted as a late arrival joined us.

'I'm shattered,' she exclaimed, 'utterly exhausted.' 'You haven't been far,' said one girl. 'Ah but I practically had to do the flight single-handed. Poor Belinda was with me today, she has gone home now, not at all well, trouble with her 'you know what' (patting her tummy). Bad pain, flooding, you name it. I did at least 80% of the work.'

'She has awfully long periods,' said Ursula dryly. 'I did two flights with her this month and she was on for both of those.'

Two girls chorused together, 'but the same happened with us,' 'and with me too,' said a third voice, which was followed by silence. 'We are being had,' Ursula calmly announced. 'I've counted five periods this month so far.' With that something clicked into place in all our heads, something we hadn't quite been able to put our finger on since Belinda had joined Starways nine months earlier.

She was a very nice girl, slim figure, pretty face, blue eyes and light brown hair. The only extraordinary thing about Belinda was her complete lack of temperament. She just did not have one, along with no cigarettes, no make-up, no money and nobody to look after her which she assumed everyone had a duty to do.

The 'Miss' on her passport was incorrect. She was a 'Mrs' and on a first trip with Belinda we were all told of the wicked husband who had gone off and left her penniless. To a man we all felt the urge to protect and defend this poor girl that fate had dealt such a blow. A trip with Belinda was never a hassle as long as one was prepared to do the work. She would stand shyly on one side as our Traffic Manager gave us last-minute orders.

As we walked out to the aircraft she always queried 'what would you like me to do first?' She smiled widely as each passenger boarded the aircraft.

Then it began, as we sat side by side for take-off, first a little sigh, then a deep sigh, adding 'I don't want to be a burden to anyone but I've the most awful flooding just now. Could I, er, just pour the drinks and hand you the passengers' lunches? It really would be embarrassing if I did too much walking about.'

Any suggestion that she get medical help and advice was met with, 'oh, I'm too embarrassed,' and 'it always seems to clear up when I book a doctor's appointment.'

And so a trip with Belinda began that way for us all. She continually smoked throughout the trip and the cigarettes she smoked were always yours. Duty Free cigarettes on board were 1/- a packet (5p), but she never bought one until we were on finals for our destination. She would take maybe two strolls through the cabin with the crew's tea and as she passed by, whisper, 'I'm taking their tea up – for you!'

One felt she was doing the biggest favour in the world. On reaching anywhere, Belinda would ask in a soft voice 'shall I go to the restaurant and order your lunch for you?' As the last passenger descended the steps so her words came. In her condition one could hardly say 'no.'

So, alone, you checked the catering and drinks order for the return trip; you straightened the seat belts and as you did so, the crew would pass through the cabin and ask, 'how's poor Belinda? Is she feeling better now?' The Captain often added – 'don't be too long coming over, I want a quick turnaround if we can manage it.'

GLORIA

GLORIA had had an excellent education, spoke

three languages, and was an ex-nursing sister and midwife. She was also the correct height for a model, had a wonderful figure and a lovely heart-shaped face. In 1960 she was also the only girl in Starways to own a car and in her wardrobe were more clothes than the rest of us had put together.

She had everything but good eyesight and a sense of humour. And the former was a secret she managed to keep to herself, occasionally with contact lenses which made her eyes sore. So 75% of the time Gloria made her way blindly from the traffic office to the aircraft and once on board she would don her specs on the pretext of checking paperwork.

Sunny days saw Gloria blossom, her lightly-tinted sunglasses were prescription lenses. On those days we all remarked on her good humour little knowing the reason why. On the cloudy days most folk completely recoiled as our 'Hi's' and 'Hello's' were met with a stony, blank stare. It was an unfounded fear of losing her job that led to Gloria confiding in no-one and so building a barrier between us.

Gloria and I had crewed many an uneventful flight and the flight we had just completed to South Africa was equally uneventful. The crew were to spend two days in Johannesburg and as we departed for their hotel I was excited because I'd been given permission to stay with my sister for two days.

My sister Barbara and her husband had lived in

Johannesburg for three years as he was with South African Airways, and we hadn't met during that time. Now, with my brother-in-law away on a trip, my sister and I spent our time sightseeing, visiting her friends and chatting.

We were exhausted with delight at seeing each other – so much so that we found it hard to sleep at night. Those two days just flew by and soon the morning of departure for me dawned and, as the alarm by the bed exploded into life, I opened my weary eyes.

Putting her arm around me, my sister muttered 'we'll get up in a minute,' and with that we both fell back into a deep sleep. I awoke with a start, 40 minutes before our aircraft's scheduled departure time from Jan Smuts airport, Johannesburg. Panic was not the word, I was almost hysterical!

I phoned the crew's hotel to find they had departed for the airport two hours ago. Still unwashed, I threw my uniform on, my sister meanwhile tried to contact the crew at the airport but couldn't reach them as they had already boarded the aircraft.

Now tearful, I had visions of being left behind and worse being dismissed on my eventual return to Liverpool. I heard my sister speaking and looking at her through my tears she mouthed the words 'Police.'

Within minutes, not only had she summoned up a police car but with it came a motorcycle escort. I remember very little of the journey – how far it was or how long it took, only the speedometer of the car waving between 90 and 100 miles per hour, the wailing sirens and the unemotional police who drove me straight onto the tarmac and pulled up at the steps of our aircraft.

Dishevelled, I thanked them as graciously as possible and climbed the aircraft steps to meet the thunder of our Captain's face. He had spent the last half an hour making arrangements for me to fly back to London with BOAC (British Overseas Airways Corporation).

True to the nature of aircrews, two hours into our flight, all was forgiven and we happily settled down to the long journey home. Our passengers were 82 Cambridge students. They had been in South Africa for three months on an educational trip and were returning home stony broke but happy.

Our aircraft cabin was full to bursting with tribal spears, drums, bows and arrows and heaven knows what other weapons. As hijacking was completely unknown in those days no-one bothered to remove the weapons from their owners and the aircraft took on a festive air. These passengers were a delight to look after, jokes and ad-libbing were rife, meals were hilarious and laughter abounded.

By the time we reached Kano in Nigeria we felt as though we knew each and every one of them and they felt they knew us. Gloria's lack of humour was targeted mercilessly. The more serious she was, the more these young devils enjoyed themselves. After a night stop in Nigeria we departed early the following evening and dinner and drinks were served immediately after take-off.

At around 11pm the cabin lights were dimmed for the passengers to sleep and I was told by Faith (No.1 Stewardess) to take a two-hour rest. Back into the cabin I went and sat in the only seat available next to one of the students. This young man appeared not a bit sleepy and began a conversation the moment I sat down.

After a while I asked him about Cambridge. 'Oh, I'm not from Cambridge,' he said, smiling. 'There are six of us on board from the School of Speech and Drama, I'm going to be an actor someday so remember my name Gary Bond.' He was an extremely good-looking 21-year-old with a delight-ful sense of humour and with such confidence and enthusiasm about what he was going to do in life. I felt like a mother hen listening to his dreams.

We were deep in conversation when I saw the shadowy figure of Faith making her way through the cabin towards me. 'Can you come forward,' she whispered. I made my excuses to Gary and fol-lowed Faith to the galley.

Once inside, her eyes met mine and she raised her eyebrows towards heaven. 'We,' she paused, 'have a major oil leak on No.2 engine and are returning to Kano, this will take about three hours.' Turning to Gloria and me, she added, 'don't tell the passengers just yet, let them sleep.'

Nigeria was in the throes of its independence

celebrations as we landed for the second time. A skeleton staff of expatriates had seen us depart and the same few greeted our return along with African employees who were the worse for drink.

The place was shambolic. The hotels were full of visitors attending the celebrations, most Africans were drunk and now us, with an injured aircraft and 90 more bodies to find shelter and food for only added to the confusion.

We were told that things fuelled by alcohol had heated up that night. Among other incidents a teacher's car had been turned over and set alight causing one death and most of the British were very concerned that things could get worse.

Luck, though, was very much on our side as a nearby RAF base agreed to house the crew plus 20 passengers while the remaining passengers were found hotel accommodation next to the airport. We three girls were taken to the bungalow of an RAF officer and his wife for what was to be one night. It turned out to be five days!

It was on our second night's stay when the RAF couple decided to throw a party for us. They asked the Captain to bring 20 of our passengers as well as the crew. Among those who came were young Gary Bond and a friend of his called Robere. During the evening they came over and talked to me – then Gary, with a twinkle in his eye and a nudge into my ribs, said 'how's your acting ability?'

'What acting ability?' I gave him a puzzled look. 'Let's see what you can do, as we want to have a bit of a giggle.' Sounding every bit like a director, he continued, 'what you have to do is dance with me, gaze the whole time into my eyes and talk. It doesn't matter what you talk about, you can say "rhubarb, rhubarb, rhubarb" but don't take your eyes from mine for a second – look lovingly and longingly but whatever you do, don't laugh.

He placed his hand on my arm. 'Now, this is the plan, after a few minutes Robere will come along, tap you on the shoulder, then you dance with him in exactly the same way. Remember, loving and longing and for heaven's sake don't laugh.' 'What are you up to?' I queried. 'Don't ask questions,' answered Gary, 'be a sport and let's see how good

an actress you are.' He then left me and returned to a far corner of the room.

As a romantic melody drifted across the room from the record player, Gary approached me and our dance began – first Gary, then

Patsy was no stranger to the stage – here she is after she had taken part in a show with the Norbury Revue Co, aged 26, in 1962.

Robere, Gary, then Robere and so we continued until I was just about to say to one of them, 'how long are we going to play this game for?' when I saw a stern-looking Gloria making her way towards me through the dancers.

'Can I have a word with you?' she said, inches from my face. I opened my eyes wide, realising what the boys' game was. 'Not here.' Gloria nodded towards the corner of the room. I left Gary and followed her. 'You,' she continued, 'are going to cause trouble if you carry on like that.' I was just about to say it was only a joke when across the room I spied Gary and Robere waiting with a drink for me and grinning from ear to ear. The devils! I shook my head and smiled back realising they were only having sport with Gloria's lack of humour – she, by then, had turned on her heels and departed in a huff.

On our way back to Liverpool four days later, the tables were turned as Gloria justifiably got a laugh at my expense. We made a fuel stop in Casablanca. The passengers remained on board; we hoped to be on the ground for the shortest time possible.

I was by the main cabin door when Gloria came. 'You've got to collect your things together and report to the Captain on the double,' she said as I entered the cockpit. The Captain was looking studiously at some papers. He didn't look up but grunted, 'Miss Collins I find we are overweight for take-off in this heat so I am having to off-load you.

'That aircraft over there,' he pointed through the

cockpit window, 'is going to London and the skipper has agreed to carry you. He's a little faster than us so you'll arrive at Heathrow first, so wait in the Starways traffic office until our arrival.'

I said goodbye and trundled down the aircraft steps with all my personal belongings. I noticed Casablanca's airport was full of military personnel heavily armed and accompanied by Alsatian dogs. I crossed the tarmac to the appointed aircraft's steps, a journey of not more than 300 yards.

I was then stopped from ascending the aircraft steps by an armed guard and my pleas to board the aircraft were useless as it was obvious he didn't understand a word of English. I could not understand him so another armed officer arrived and spoke to me in French, ashamedly I didn't understand him either.

Suddenly a member of the aircraft's crew came down the steps and began speaking to me in a completely unrecognisable language and by this time we had been joined by two more armed guards all talking and arguing amongst themselves. Four pairs of beady Alsatian eyes were giving us all an old-fashioned look. Feeling completely bewildered, I looked up and saw another man appear in the cabin doorway.

From the top of the aircraft steps he started what I can only assume was a shouting conversation with the crew member at the bottom. This continued for at least five minutes during which time I tried to recognise the language.

Another chap now appeared in the cabin door-way. He looked down at me, 'are you English?' he asked, firmly. With a grateful smile and great relief I answered 'yes!' 'Wait,' he said, and disappeared into the cabin. I waited, trying to avoid the eyes of the armed guards not to mention the Alsatians who had all become silent.

With some relief I heard movement on the steps again as a heavily gold-braided, distinguished-looking man descended towards me. As he reached the bottom his hand stretched out towards mine. 'Madam,' he paused, 'may I be of assistance to you?' I began to tell my story 'and so you see,' I ended, 'this is the aircraft I'm returning to London in.'

He was completely silent for a few moments. 'Then you are a British Stewardess?' he queried, 'with what Company?' 'Starways,' I answered, 'Starways of Liverpool.' 'This Company I do not know,' he answered coolly. 'But I do know this aircraft is not travelling to London, we are return-ing to Moscow.'

I opened my mouth to speak but couldn't think of what to say. As the penny dropped, I realised I'd been had. The pigs – how rotten, I could have been imprisoned, was all I could think. I mumbled something apologetic and turned towards our Skymaster. My humour gone and feeling quite weepy and silly I climbed the aircraft steps, a handkerchief dabbing my eyes as I entered the cabin to deafening applause from 80 laughing

Cambridge students all enjoying the joke enormously and patting my back on the walk through the cabin to galley and cockpit.

'Where have you been?' There stood an innocent-looking crew, smiling. 'That wasn't funny,' I mumbled crossly. They smiled again. 'We expected you back within 30 seconds but you did make rather a meal of it, where's your sense of humour?' said Gloria. 'No comment!' I replied.

The front of Faith's bungalow in Liverpool looked out onto Sefton Park. Its large garden was mostly lawn and large, shady trees. Ropes hung from tree to tree, festooned daily with newly-washed bras and panties and other girly things. The bungalow's lattice windows seemed to be permanently open and the sounds of Ray Conniff, Ella Fitzgerald and Johnny Mathis were heard continually as Ursula played her half-dozen LPs over and over again.

Faith, a little older than us, was delightful to live with. As a landlady she resembled a Fairy Godmother. As a friend she was the best. Her house was open to all. She observed everything with a smile and judged no-one. When funds were low, she fed us and when spirits were low she cheered us. She herself was not happily married and her husband was barely civil to us but in retrospect one can hardly blame him. It was his home and to have noisy stewardesses all over the house must have been very tiring, even exasperating.

Cedric had a white poodle called Maxi – one of the most aggressive dogs anyone could meet. He had a horrible habit of jumping onto our eating table and spread-eagling himself there and not moving.

From left: Faith with Maxi on her lap, Patsy in the middle and Ursula on the right. Taken in Faith's house, where Ursula and Patsy rented a room.

All our attempts to coax him off were met with snarling teeth and growling. Only two people could remove Maxi from the table – Cedric, with one click of his fingers the dog would jump down, and Faith – when Cedric was away, she would get a broom and use the long handle to smartly push Maxi onto the floor.

We had a 'be nice to Cedric' week once. We usually took turns to cook our main daily meal. That week we tried to cook all his favourite dishes but each meal was met with stony silence. After our best efforts, which brought praise indeed from us girls, Faith's husband just ate all before him and without so much as a nod or a thank you, left the table.

On the last day Ursula, who, being so glamorous, kept her cooking skills a secret but was in fact a superb cook, produced a most delicious brunch. Maxi, seated on the table, refused to move. Cedric appeared, reading a paper in one hand and without looking up. He clicked his fingers with the other and the dog jumped down.

Dettol cloth in hand, I wiped the table and laid it as Ursula put plates of her delicious brunch down before us. A stony-faced Cedric slowly lowered his paper and said, 'I don't eat cremated sausages,' and with that rose and walked to the door. To stop Ursula throwing a full plate of food at him, I mentioned to her that we had nowhere to go if he threw us out.

CHAPTER SIX

RUSTY

DURING the 1950s and 1960s, London Airport – as Heathrow was then known – was a small, friendly place. We got to know many airport staff personally.

One young man who was always around when we landed was called 'Rusty'. He was with Airport Services. Rusty would assist us with any request. He'd drive us to and from our aircraft and do any job he was asked. We all became extremely fond of him and he was obviously extremely fond of us.

He started to greet us with small gifts and these presents became daily treats. We all became embarrassed by the gifts as we knew he wasn't highly paid. But against our wishes he continued with his kindness and we tried hard to repay him. This went on for a year or more until one day, Rusty was missing and nobody at the Airport seemed to know where he was.

Time passed and no Rusty, until one day we heard that he had died. We missed seeing him dreadfully. He had become so much part of our landing in London. Many months later, we were told he died of starvation. We never found out if he was anorexic or just couldn't afford food. The news of how he died was just too painful to contemplate.

Fifty years later his death still fills my heart with sadness for his wasted young life. His smile, eagerness to please and a memory of Rusty standing shyly with a small gift in his hand, will never be forgotten. For some reason he loved us, and we all loved him.

Rusty with Fay, left, and Patsy, right, at Heathrow Airport

CHAPTER SEVEN

AMERICAN ADVENTURE

URSULA and I could get free flights to the USA through our airline. So in October 1962, we decided to have our first real holiday and travel the United States together. I had an Auntie Anne in California so that is where we decided to go.

We saved for many months and finally had enough money for a 99-dollar Greyhound Bus ticket. This ticket was only available in the UK to encourage tourists to the States. And we were told all airline staff had half-price concessions throughout the USA's hotels and motels.

So, armed with our tickets plus £50 Sterling, we set off on our adventure. We took a Starways flight to London and a Pan American flight to Miami, Florida. Having seen only Hollywood films it was like a dream to set foot on American soil. But Florida Customs officers brought us down to earth. They were positively rude as they quizzed us about why we were in the USA and when they suggested it could be for immoral purposes, we were so insulted we nearly came home.

We had no intention of staying in Florida so headed straight to the Greyhound Bus Station for a bus to Alabama, Louisiana, and made New Orleans our first stop-over.

We arrived to find the bus station like World War II – it was manic. There was an air of panic and people rushing about everywhere.

We were totally lost and confused until we were finally told that Cuba was about to invade Florida, and it seemed as though everyone was trying to leave the State. We had arrived just as the Cuban missile crisis was starting which nearly led to war between the Soviet Union and the United States.

By now extremely tired and nearly crushed to death, I mouthed: 'what shall we do?' to Ursula. 'Well, I'm not staying here with this lot,' she answered. Anyway, we said together, 'we are British, we're not running away.'

'Let's find a hotel,' said I. Ursula replied, with her typical Liverpool humour: 'Anyway, I fancy Castro!'

The hotels we tried wouldn't take us as they had no staff – everyone had deserted their jobs. A police officer suggested we try Miami Beach. To our delight The Fontaine Bleue – without staff but with a kind hotel manager – agreed to give us a room. We would have to look after ourselves, but we were so grateful to have a bed and shower.

At 7pm we had a call from the manager asking if we would like a little cold supper. We were famished and joined him in the restaurant. 'We have two other guests with us and they will join us shortly,' said the manager.

Can you imagine our surprise when the singer Mel Tormé and another man came to the table? Apparently Mel Tormé was the cabaret at the hotel for that week and his companion was his manager and they had decided not to take flight. He did a show for us that evening. And for the next three nights we were all together and they were all gentlemen and wonderful company.

When it was time to say goodbye, the manager shook our hands but refused to take any money for our stay. 'Just tell your passengers this is a great place to stay,' he said, warmly.

Soviet-backed Cuba and the USA never did go to war, of course, so two well-rested, well-fed and now golden-tanned girls boarded a bus for New Orleans. We slept on the bus until we reached the city where it was hot, humid and sticky. We found a cheap motel by the bus station and planned to stay two nights. We showered and ventured out to find something to eat. As we stepped out that early evening, the pavement appeared to move. Ursula retreated back into the motel with, 'I am not going out there!'

'We have to eat,' I said.

I set foot on the pavement which was moving with what turned out to be cockroach-type bugs which crunched under my feet as I made my way towards a small shop. There I purchased fresh bread, cheese and oranges. Unhappy about staying, we caught a bus going west with our remaining food as a picnic. Our next stop was Lubbock in

Texas. We stepped out to clear blue skies and amazingly polite Texans. Stetson-hatted males over six-feet tall said, 'howdy Ma'am,' and 'Morning, Ma'am' and asked to be of service. We were helped to our hotel with a raised hat and a bow.

After a delightful two days we boarded our west-bound Greyhound Bus. The bus was full of young people and buzzing with laughter and chat. It did not take us long to join in the merry-making. We didn't get a wink's sleep as they continually sang, 'Deep in the Heart of Texas'. Everyone shared their food and drink. The moon and stars seemed so big I watched them in awe.

Around midnight, Ursula remembered we had a half-bottle of whiskey. Into the plastic cups on board she poured a small tot topped with fresh orange juice and we passed these around. We were all enjoying our meagre drink when the bus came to an abrupt halt. The driver left his seat and walked down the aisle of our dimly-lit coach. He stopped halfway down. He glared at all of us and said, 'someone's drinkin' on ma bus and if Ah find out who it is, they'll go to jail.'

Ursula, her drink untouched, dropped the whole thing on the floor as the driver returned to his seat.

Our only comfort-stop was 'Flagstaff Arizona' before we reached Las Vegas. In 1962, Las Vegas was little more than a strip in the desert. We only saw two hotels, The Sands and The Thunderbird next door to each other. We stayed in The Thunderbird and they charged us a pittance. The sole reason we were staying in Vegas was to meet Frank Sinatra. We had heard so much about him in the UK we thought he lived at The Sands. So we were disappointed to find he had been there the week before but had now left.

During the days of our four-day stop we walked the dusty strip and ate the wonderful cheap food and every night we sat in The Sands hotel nursing our one drink, and getting to know the staff while listening in awe to their tales of Sinatra. On our last night we asked for mementoes and were given two ashtrays, a cruet set and some coasters. Finally, the barman came over to our table and said, 'you girls leaven' tomorrow?' We nodded. 'Well wait until we close and we'll grab you a table and four chairs to take with you,' he said, jokingly. At that point, we stopped asking!

We had observed through Florida, Alabama, Louisiana and Texas that coloured folk only sat in the last two rows at the back of the bus. So we decided for the rest of our journey that that was where we would sit. We boarded our bus and sat at the very back. A couple of coloured folk got on and were obviously uncomfortable sitting near us. When the driver noticed he marched to the back of the bus and said, 'you girls move forward, please.' In our very best English we said, 'we like these seats.' He replied: 'You'll have to move, these seats are for niggers.'

'Oh, is that the law?' we said. 'No, ma'am, it's the

done thing.' Well, we replied, 'if we are not breaking the law we will stay here.' And we did, all the way to Los Angeles and we got very funny looks from passengers.

At Los Angeles, my Auntie Anne met us at the bus station. She had a car with the driving seat removed and replaced with an armchair-like contraption – placed rather unstably, we found out on our journey to her home in Woodland Hills. Thankfully the back seat was fine, and we watched our luggage wobble in front beside Anne who laughed all the way home.

We had an amazing week with Anne, her husband and children Janet, Margaret and Douglas. Anne, a teacher, had worked for Fred Hope (Bob Hope's brother). She took us on a private visit to the 20th Century Fox Location Ranch with its many towns, railway stations, airports and palaces. It seemed as vast as the UK. We had tickets for The Diana Shaw Show and met her, plus actor Jack Lemmon and actress and dancer Cyd Charisse. At another show we met actors Danny Kaye, Doris Day and Charlton Heston. We went to every famous spot in Hollywood and Beverly Hills, even to the stage of the Hollywood Bowl.

Our last night was spent having dinner with a Hollywood director and his English wife who told us how well-known stars were desperate to find honest help as the Mexican girls willing to take domestic jobs were controlled by their boyfriends who wanted access to famous people's houses. He told us that British girls could make a fortune. I was tempted and completely star-struck. But Ursula, newly-engaged, was in love and couldn't wait to get home.

Our return to Miami was the fastest 3,000 miles

Airgirls' 6,000 Miles By Bus

Ursula Larson (left) and Pat Collins.

Two Liverpool air hostesses are back home after one of their longest-ever trips — 6,000 miles across America by bus.

Pat Collins and Ursula Larson, both aged 26, of 100 Score Lane, Childwall, who fly for Starways, decided that they would pack as much sight-seeing into their month's holiday as they possibly could.

They flew from London to Miami—on a concession rate for the air passage, of course — and then started the marathon trip which took them to New Orleans, El Paso, Los Angeles, Las Vegas, Fort Worth, Mexico and Hollywood.

They met several film stars including Dan Dailey, Jack Lemmon, Cyd Charisse and several members of the cast of television's "Bonanza" series.

"We hoped to see Frank Sinatra but were unlucky," said Pat. "We were on the bus for a fortnight altogether but it was far from boring. There was so much to see."

Said Ursula: "It was wonderful."

Cost of the trip? About £80 each.

Patsy and Ursula's trip made a story for the Liverpool Echo at the time.

ever – we slept and ate on the bus and arrived exhausted the night before our flight. Our money had run out two days before so we slept at the bus station. By the time we boarded our flight we were so hungry we couldn't think.

We told one of the stewardesses of our plight and she gave us bags of crisps and nuts until the meals were ready. Then we had two dinners each and fell asleep, only waking for breakfast before landing in London, where we took a Starways flight home to Liverpool.

For all the wonderful sights we had witnessed, when we saw the Widnes Bridge and the Mersey River on the final approach to Liverpool, we knew where our hearts belonged.

CHAPTER EIGHT

THE MANAGEMENT

THE stewardesses' relationship with the Starways management one could say, honestly didn't exist! An occasional 'Good morning Miss,' came our way as we proceeded from traffic office to aircraft but mostly our male bosses, with all the problems of running an airline and keeping it solvent had little, if any, thought for their £6-per-week girls who worked all the hours God sent.

How we kept ourselves attractive, paid our rent and ate, out of our meagre wages was a miracle. Many weeks, the money left for feeding ourselves was non-existent. We ate, of course, as much as we could on duty and supplemented home food by collecting the left-over portions of silver-wrapped cheese and apples from the passengers' lunch boxes. This, with crusty bread, made a surprisingly good meal on days off.

On our Liverpool-London-Liverpool early morning flights our passengers were offered tea, coffee or fruit juice. Invariably they had tea or coffee so the tomato, orange or grapefruit juices provided another source of free nourishment for us.

There was rarely a vacant seat on these flights so time was short and we often didn't get a drink during the flight. On these days we disembarked with a tin of juice in our handbag. It was after one such flight that I was asked to report to the General Manager's Office. As I crossed the tarmac to the hangar offices I met a rather puzzled Ronnie English who was in charge of catering.

As I explained where I was going Ronnie turned ashen. 'Oh Lord,' he said, 'I thought so-and-so was on that flight, she's so rude to us, we decided to do a spot check. Why are you here?' he added.

'So-and-so is sick and I was on standby,' I replied. 'Patsy, I'm sorry.' Ronnie put his hand on my arm and looked soulful. 'We reported cans of fruit juice missing. We did it to teach her a lesson – she's such a madam and so rude to the ground staff, but if I'd known you were the hostie . . .'

'It doesn't matter,' I replied as the hangar loomed before me. Because of our quick London turnaround all our rubbish bins had been emptied back in Liverpool so if we, or passengers, had drunk the juice the empties would be in the bin. Ronnie looked so glum I put a friendly hand on his shoulder and marched in to meet my fate. Captain Leigh was busy so I sat outside his office for what seemed like hours.

Suddenly a gruff, 'I'll see Miss Collins now,' came through the open door and his secretary nodded for me to go in. The lump in my throat settled with a bump into my tummy as I entered the brightly neon-lit office. Captain Leigh didn't even raise his head. As I stood there he continued to sign papers and answer telephone calls without so much as a glance in my direction.

Eventually I could bear it no longer. 'You wanted to see me, Sir?' I croaked, then cleared my throat. Still concentrating on the papers he announced to the desk 'some tins of fruit juice are missing from your aircraft, do you happen to know where they are?'

'Yes Sir, I have one and Miss Batstone has the other.' 'And do you usually steal company property?' he asked, looking up for the first time with a steely gaze. 'We usually drink what's left of the opened cans,' I replied.

'I'm talking about removing company property.'

'Yes, yes sometimes,' I muttered. 'So you took one and Miss Batstone took one?' 'No, Sir, that's not the way it was. I took one and gave one to Corrine and she was worried about taking it.' The two minutes' silence that followed were purgatory. I seemed to sway almost as though I was drunk as I tried to stand still.

He broke the silence. 'You realise this is stealing?' 'No Sir, I didn't.'

Another silence followed. I was now desperate to go to the loo. 'I will have to suspend you, Miss Collins – for one month and if there is a next time, you will be dismissed. You may go.'

I turned and reached for the door and was halted by 'one moment, Miss, don't think you are suspended to sit at home washing your blouses, do you know how to operate a switchboard?' 'No Sir.'

'Well, now's your time to learn. Report to my secretary at 0900 hours tomorrow.'

Looking on the switchboard punishment as a challenge and so relieved and happy not to be sacked from the job I loved, I arrived cheerfully at 0900 the next day. But by lunchtime I was almost demented and near to tears. Having no time to master the switchboard, we had been inundated with a succession of continental and transatlantic calls and harassed to breaking point.

I had now become so confused. All the offices were engaged when at noon an important call came through for our Commercial Manager, Mr Johnson. It was France's third attempt to get him and now they wished to hold until he was free. Checking his engaged line again, I accidentally cut someone else off and they buzzed me back, confusion was now rife and I accidentally cut the Technical Director (Cliff Gates) off, his constant buzzing had sent me into a panic. This time he shouted 'what the hell are you doing, Miss Collins?'

With that, I burst into tears and informed him that if they wanted an efficient switchboard operator they should get one and with that I pulled out all the telephone plugs and sat there waiting for someone to give me the sack.

Thankfully, Captain Leigh was away that day as that might well have been my fate. Instead, Mr Gates, who had done all the buzzing and shouting that morning arrived like the Angel Gabriel and sat with me for two hours, patiently instructing as each call came in. By noon I was a competent switch-board operator.

Captain Leigh seldom flew because his commit-ments as General Manager were so heavy, but once a month he did a flight to keep his licence valid. On my first flight after the switchboard saga, Captain Leigh flew the Liverpool-Gatwick leg of a flight to Majorca. The Starways Dakotas took their time to get to London so it was always a rather relaxed flight with plenty of chatting to passengers as teas, coffees, etc, were served.

Twenty minutes before landing I got into deep conversation with the couple on the rear seat as I stacked away washed dishes. The male passenger suddenly asked me if he could have half a bottle of brandy. I explained how the law didn't allow us to open a duty free bar until we had left the UK. 'As soon as we leave Gatwick the first half will be yours, Sir.' I smiled, 'sorry.'

We now began descending into cloud and the seatbelt sign came on. As the aircraft swayed in the mild turbulence I began my cabin walk to check the passengers were safely strapped in. As I neared the rear seat again I heard a choking sound. Lifting my eyes from seatbelts I saw my 'half bottle of brandy' passenger gasping for breath.

A second later I loosened his tie, collar, trouser belt – anything, in fact that restricted his breathing. But before I had finished I realised he had already died. Momentarily, I froze. I knew instinctively I had to keep this from the other 36 passengers and from his wife, seated next to him. Calmly excusing myself I took no more than 60 seconds to report to Captain Leigh and return to the rear of the aircraft.

This was the first time I'd seen anyone dead and I felt a deep sadness. As I approached the back seat his wife became agitated and began to panic. 'I can't feel him breathing,' she said repeatedly. I tried to reassure her. Holding his hand, I whispered that I could feel a faint pulse and that we would be landing in a few minutes and the Captain had radioed for a doctor and ambulance. As I spoke, Captain Leigh came down the cabin towards us, took one look at the passenger and knew he'd died.

After landing, our passengers disembarked to the Transit Lounge unaware of our drama. The problem now was to get his poor wife off the aircraft. We had already been on the ground ten minutes with no sign of a doctor or ambulance but I could see two policemen at the bottom of our steps as I remained on the edge of a seat holding our dead passenger's hand. After disembarking with the passengers, Captain Leigh now returned to the aircraft with, 'I'd like a word with you, Miss.'

I followed him out of the cabin door where he told me to get the woman off as soon as possible, or he would deal with it himself. 'I can't feel him breathing,' said his wife, tragically, as I returned to their seat. Taking his wrist in my hand and placing my head against his chest, I again announced, 'there's a faint pulse,' unable to look her in the eyes.

'Oh dear,' I continued, 'they are a long time

coming, I was going to ask you a favour but I can't because you are a passenger, you see. I will have to stay until the doctor arrives.'

'Go on dear, what is it?' She put her hand on mine. 'I'd love a sandwich and fresh tea. If you go and get yourself a drink you could order one for me too.' Bless her, she got up and the last I saw of her was a smile from the cabin doorway.

No sooner had she left than about five policemen boarded the aircraft; one examined our dead passenger whilst another questioned me. 'Did you inform the passenger that the aircraft had lost an engine?' he queried. Bewildered, I told him I was unaware we had lost an engine. 'When did the Captain inform you?' 'Ah, he didn't.' 'Did any of the passengers appear shocked?' 'No, we were chatting about a half bottle of brandy, everything was normal when he just died.'

Captain Leigh now appeared in the cabin door-way. 'Excuse me, Sir, I didn't even know we'd lost an engine.' 'What engine?' He looked at the police and informed them that Derby Aviation had lost an engine and had made an emergency landing request only moments before our request for a doctor and ambulance. The police having been informed thought we were one and the same aircraft.

After 20 minutes the doctor arrived from Horley and pronounced our poor passenger dead. As they began to remove the body the doctor approached me. 'How are you feeling, young lady?' he asked.

Had I seen anyone die before? Did I feel fit enough to travel on to Palma? One look past the doctor to Captain Leigh's face told me I'd better be ok.

I smiled at the doctor reassuringly and convinced him I was fine, even though I felt sick. We all disembarked as the ambulance drove away. The doctor said he'd given the chap's wife an injection and she was ok but I felt I had let her down in some way. Captain Leigh and the doctor left me at the aircraft steps and I saw my next crew come into view.

'Wish we were Chinese,' said Captain Hammond as he passed me. 'Oh I wish I was Chinese too.' repeated FO Frank Carroll. I looked at them as they rubbed their hands together and didn't smile. 'We then could all celebrate him going to his ancestors,' added Don. I smiled as I shook my head – they were trying to cheer me up, which was just as well as behind them our passengers came into view.

Amazingly, we landed in Majorca only one-and-a-half hours late. As I made my way through Palma Airport Terminal Building I came face to face with F H Wilson, our Chairman and owner of Starways.

'Hello, Miss er, er, er, er, why are you so late?' he stammered. 'We had a passenger die between Liverpool and Gatwick, Sir!' He looked at his watch, then at me again. 'And did that delay you a whole hour and a half?' he asked, crossly. I looked at him open-mouthed as Don and Frank, now behind me, gave me a little push in my back.

'We,' said Captain Hammond, 'are going to the

restaurant for a meal.' So, completely ignoring F H Wilson, they walked on.

A funny anecdote to this story I only learnt on my return to Liverpool. Our dead passenger's 'wife' turned out not to be his wife. They were on a secret holiday and his real wife was back in Liverpool. At Gatwick the girlfriend had been more worried about items of her clothing which were in his suitcase than the fact that the poor chap had died. Captain Leigh and his FO spent over three hours sorting her problem out.

The doctor said there was nothing I could have done to save our heart attack passenger, which was a relief. Inside me there still remained the niggling thought – could I have done more? I hoped I'd never have to experience that again.

But less than a month later, on a Viscount flight to Pisa, Paddy and I had just finished serving lunch and coffees to our 76 passengers and were taking a 10-minute break for milk and a cigarette when a woman came rushing to us from the middle of the cabin. 'My husband's sick,' she shouted, 'his heart.'

As I went forward this was confirmed as I saw him gasping for breath. I motioned to Paddy to take the wife and daughter to the back of the aircraft whilst loosening every article of clothing on him. Paddy came back with oxygen as I lifted the arm rests and laid him across the three seats.

Then, kneeling down with his head resting on my right arm and the oxygen mask in my left hand,

I thought I would silently pray for him not to die. 'Please God, don't let this one die. You just cannot die, not again – I won't let you,' I whispered.

We kept the wife and daughter in our seats at the rear of the aircraft and I stayed with our sick passenger until we landed in Pisa. By now he'd made a remarkable recovery and didn't want any fuss but we, of course, notified the courier who said he would take him for a medical check.

'Goodbye Sir! Please take care,' I said, as he walked to the cabin door and began to leave our aircraft. He smiled, 'I wouldn't dare do anything else after the amount of times you ordered me not to die.'

It was the winter of 1961 and Christmas was drawing near. Our meagre wages now seemed to be

Patsy's still smiling after a Pisa to Palma night flight.

buying less and less. Our families would not be getting any festive presents from us this year so in desperation five of us girls decided to go carol singing. Complete with Liverpool University scarves (donated by Paddy) and a money tin reading 'HOSFAM' we set off to the Aigburth district of Liverpool.

Snow was on the ground but wasn't very deep. It was a clear, frosty night; the starry sky was magnificent but there was a bitterly cold wind. Not having the luxury of fur boots we tripped through Prince's Park in our working high heels hardly able to feel our frozen feet.

Singing, as we thought, like angels, our tin's takings soared to 15 shillings in no time and our hearts became lighter. Then we came to the first door of a large house off Lark Lane. To the strains of 'Silent Night' the door was opened by a large gentleman.

With the hallway's bright light shining in our eyes we could just see his outline. When we finished he pressed half a crown into a willing hand and requested another carol. We thanked him and burst into 'Oh, Come All Ye Faithful.' 'What are you girls collecting for?' This surprise question came with our carol's last note. Someone blurted out 'HOSFAM' and the rest of us stood open-mouthed. 'Well done, well done, good girls. Are any of you on tomorrow morning's London flight?'

'Yes,' someone stuttered. 'And you still find time to help a charity.' He took his wallet out of his trouser pocket and removed a £1 note. Still unable to see his face we were now feeling quite ill at ease as he pushed the note into a hand and wished us 'Merry Christmas.'

As soon as he closed the door, we all began to run and we ran without stopping all the way back to my flat in Linnet Lane where, to thaw us out, I heated my only bottle of red wine and made a punch which they said tasted like 'Parish's food' – a well-known tonic. Two eggs scrambled with milk made a meal for four and as we sat around the table slowly defrosting and devouring our feast, we decided we couldn't risk another night's singing for the 'Hostess Famine Society.'

There was nothing else for it, (with our heads full of punch), we decided to plan a strike. Getting together a meeting of Charter airline staff who are invariably dispersed to different parts of the world at any one time is nothing short of a miracle. That was the major stumbling block we finally overcame in early spring. With London, Glasgow and Amsterdam flights just in and a Paris and Hamburg about to depart, we managed a girls' meeting long enough to make a plan.

Betty said it wouldn't be fitting for her to take part as she was on the management side, but she agreed to help in any way possible as her wages were as low as ours. And she asked me to be a volunteer spokesman.

The following week I spent every spare moment at Betty's Mum's house in Garston. We knew that to be effective, our strike had to be unanimous. None of us felt very happy about it. We loved our jobs and were genuinely frightened of losing them and hoped it wouldn't come to a strike, as all we wanted was a small rise - £1 maybe £2 a week.

After scrutinising our programmes for the month ahead we finally earmarked a Friday evening when every aircraft would be departing: 6pm was strike time. We would down tools when all our internal flights had landed and the aircraft were about to disperse to many foreign parts.

That Friday evening at 16.30 I sat in the airport lounge allegedly scheduled to take off on a continental weekend. Clutching a folder with the precious notes of our imminent surprise strike I felt nervous as I waited for the others to arrive. Still alone, I sipped my now cold tea as I glanced yet again towards the departure lounge door and this time, framed in the doorway, was our General Manager. Perspiration broke out on my forehead as I realised he was beckoning towards me.

Maybe he is looking for somebody else, I hoped, but as he walked towards me my brain went numb as I thought, 'Oh God, he's found out!' He then stopped halfway across the lounge and beckoned again. I got up feeling distinctly like Joan of Arc and made my way towards him.

Without a word he took hold of one of my hands and led me out of the lounge. We stopped at the top of the large marble staircase that led down to the departure terminal. I couldn't raise my head so I focussed on the wonderful brass rail that accompanied the staircase to the bottom. The sun shone brightly through the huge windows, making the brass sparkle its way down. Captain Leigh broke the silence, 'I have been hearing things, Miss Collins.'

'Have you, Sir?' I answered without looking up. He continued, 'it would be much better to discuss this sort of thing, Miss Collins, than hurt a lot of innocent people by thoughtless action.'

'We have discussed it, Sir, and the answer has always been "No." 'Well,' he said, gently, 'that's not the end of the world, not a reason to give up a fight.'

'We are not going to give up, Sir,' I interrupted. 'We plan to fight this very night.' 'What about the pilots?' he continued, ignoring my last words. 'They are fully aware that we cannot live on £6 per week,' I added. 'The engineers and all the ground staff,' he continued, 'is it their fault you are poorly paid?' 'No, Sir.' 'But you don't mind their families suffering because of this?' I opened my mouth to speak then shut it again.

'If anyone should suffer,' he said, gently, 'it should be the management, not these hard-working people.' He had put my very thoughts into words and now I was confused. I blurted out, 'we don't want to hurt anyone, Sir, but . . .'

'That's the spirit,' he interrupted and gave my hand a squeeze. 'But we do want a couple more pounds a week, we just cannot exist on our present wages.' 'I know you girls do very well to manage.' 'Well can we have a rise?' I now looked him straight in the eyes. 'Call this silly thing off', he said, 'then we'll talk about it.'

He paused as though he was going to settle things there and then. From the corner of my eye I could see some of our girls were already in the lounge. 'Sir, can you give me some sort of proposal to give the girls?' I pleaded. 'Faith, just have faith,' he replied, and with that he began descending the marble staircase.

That answer was not good enough. The girls had seen Captain Leigh and were eager to know what he had said so I repeated the conversation. 'No, it's really not good enough to call off all our plans,' I told them. 'It really is time for action and to put our plan into operation.'

The weak, half-hearted replies I now received said it all. 'Shall we postpone for a week, maybe he's telling the truth? Shall we let the Board meet first?' and so on and so on. 'It's painfully obvious this whole thing has fallen apart,' I said, bitterly, and left, making my way slowly down to the departure lounge and through the thousands of passengers. The noise was deafening; children, suitcases and harassed parents surrounded the Starways departure desk.

I continued to walk through the maze of people to the departure gate and saw Captain Leigh standing there. He smiled gently. 'Going out to check your aircraft?' 'Yes, Sir.' I couldn't smile back as the muscles on my face felt frozen. 'Good girl.' Oh how I hate him, I thought, and putting my hat firmly on my head I marched out to my aircraft with one thought: I'll get that rise if it kills me.

Even with our eventual rise of £1 per week, Ursula and I were never rich enough to run to the expense of a daily newspaper's 2½d that was also the price of a bus fare or a fresh cream doughnut and, if nothing else, we had our priorities right. Even world-shattering news escaped us so local news was non-existent. We were completely unaware of the battle Starways management were having with the main Liverpool newspapers *The Echo* and *The Daily Post*.

The management thought the airline was on the newspaper's hitlist. So on a morning Liverpool-London-Liverpool flight as we were rushing to supply our return passengers with tea, coffee and snacks etc, then wash the dishes and put them away on what was a 45-minute Viscount flight, I was stopped by the crew buzzer.

As it buzzed three to four times in quick succession I reported to the cockpit right away where our captain, James Tickle, told me our hydraulics had gone. He was hoping the First Officer could hand-pump the undercarriage down but if not we would be making an emergency landing.

Starways Liverpool to London passengers were no ordinary people. Starways had five Liverpool-London-Liverpool flights daily. They were always full with regular passengers: 99% were men. So when I made my announcement on the PA system it was to familiar faces. I looked at them as I explained our flight would land approximately 20 minutes late due to a technical fault.

Meanwhile, back near the cockpit, our FO John Morton was hand-pumping the hydraulics – these were in a small cupboard-type space next to the curtain that led into the passengers' cabin. As John's arm went backwards and forwards the curtain would rise and fall and the whole thing was visible to the first four or five rows of passengers.

As we walked through the cabin checking seatbelts we looked into the familiar faces from The Ford Motor Company, Metal Box, Hawker Siddeley, etc – many passengers were engineers of one sort or another.

'I can see the hydraulics have gone,' said one passenger, nodding towards the curtain where John was pumping away. 'Oh,' I smiled, but didn't reply. 'Who's your captain?' queried another. 'Captain Tickle,' I replied. 'Ask him if he needs any help.' Having completed the cabin check I passed on the message.

'No, we have everything under control,' said Jim. 'We'll be circling for approximately 40 more minutes to dump fuel. I'd like you seated at the main cabin door and the other stewardess by the forward door. Make sure you are strapped in but I want you to open the Main Door as soon as we touch down which may be in a field.'

I looked puzzled. 'You see,' continued Jim, 'our brakes are jammed so we may well burst a tyre or two on impact. So go back, give them all a reassuring smile, strap yourself in and cross your fingers, your legs and your eyes.'

'Jim,' I said, 'it will be fine, you're the best pilot we've got!' I actually meant those words. 'Oh God,' he said, 'give me her faith in me.'

Needless to say, Jim landed the aircraft like a mother putting down her new-born baby. Halfway along the runway we slid gently onto the grass and within 60 seconds our passengers were disembarking down portable steps with a harassed-looking Mr Gates on one side and Captain Leigh on the other.

At the terminal, the bus stopped for us all to alight. I heard a 'Hi' and there waiting by the arrival door, pencil poised over his pad was a friendly reporter. 'What went wrong?' he said, as he skipped a couple of steps to fall in with mine. 'The passengers said it was hydraulic failure and I could see you came off the runway.'

I looked at him and stopped. 'We made a superb landing and no-one was hurt, in fact most weren't aware it wasn't a normal landing until I opened the door.'

And that was all I said before marching on. Those few words were turned into an unimaginable drama and were unrecognisable when published. I was hauled before the management and landed in more trouble than I care to remember for making statements to the Press.

After the uproar had died down I asked why we couldn't be friendly to the Press and maybe get some good publicity for our airline. 'Friends – friends with the Press?' roared Captain Leigh. 'Are you mad or just plain stupid? These people haven't a friendly bone in their body. They are out for blood and with people like you helping them they don't have to go far to get it!' I stood there silently for there wasn't an answer to that negative statement.

Roy Corlette was 21 years old – a tall, red-headed boy with an extremely likeable personality. He was very conscientious and appeared to spend 20 out of 24 hours a day at the airport. He always had a smile for us and he was always waiting for something – anything at all, to happen. As a reporter for the *Echo* this was the assignment he'd been given and he was trying to do his job to the best of his ability. His job was not easy; he was hated by the Starways management, his most reasonable request was dismissed on sight and most people tried to avoid him in the first place.

The newspaper appeared to have it in for Starways but seemingly our management had it in for Roy. All of us girls befriended Roy, we felt quite sorry for him – we also had an 'if you can't fight them, join them' philosophy which we thought would pay dividends in the end.

We thought you could sensationalise anything good or bad and we were working on getting good publicity. This may have been naïve, but between the newspaper and the Starways management Roy was definitely 'piggy in the middle.' A 'piggy' who we felt was as fair-minded as a reporter could be. But for months and months our airline was front page news.

A Starways Viscount

CHAPTER NINE

CELEBRITY PASSENGERS

KEN DODD

ENTERING our cabin one early morning London flight was Ken Dodd, well-known to all Liverpudlians, however he was completely unknown to a new girl from London who viewed an eccentric-looking passenger clutching a small radio as he passed her into the cabin.

'Excuse me, Sir!' I touched his arm and he jumped in mock fright. 'Sir, please don't turn that on (I pointed to the radio, tightly clutched to his chest) while the aircraft is in flight.' 'You're not having it, no sir! You're not taking it away from me, it's mine,' he replied. Sulking like a six-year-old he hugged the radio and moved along the cabin to his seat. I saw the other stewardess smile knowingly at him but she said nothing to me.

After take-off our 45-minute Viscount flight left little time for chatty conversation with 70-odd passengers. We served the first four or five rows quickly and came to the sixth and there he was again. 'Coffee, tea or fruit juice, Sir?' I said this while still holding a tray of biscuits from the last row.

'Hot chocolate and a roast beef butty, please,' he replied, staring innocently at me. 'Sir, we only have tea or coffee.' 'Tea and a roast beef butty, please,' he replied. I passed the tea. 'Sir, we don't have any sandwiches on this flight, only biscuits.'

'Biscuits?' He looked at the tray I offered him. 'You don't have the biscuits I like,' he said, seriously, 'the ones my mother gave me.' 'Sir, we have assorted biscuits, if you tell me what you like I'll pick them out for you.'

'You don't have them,' he said, sadly shaking his head. 'What are they like?' I queried. He began making funny shapes with his fingers – 'and they are black and brown.' 'What make are they?' I was now getting frustrated and could see my fellow hostess was two-thirds down the cabin working alone.

'Spillers,' he said, with a sad smile. 'Spillers,' I answered, 'ah, aren't they dog biscuits?' 'Are you insulting my mother?' I stared at him and it was only when I looked up to see the surrounding passengers laughing that I knew I'd been had.

We had many delightful flights with Ken Dodd. He genuinely is the funniest man on Earth on, or off the stage and I hope he won't mind me saying this almost 40 years later, that he asked me out many times. I now wish I'd gone, just once. We would probably have had fish and chips in Sefton Park and a lot of laughing.

THE BEATLES

WELL, I guess everybody who ever saw The Beatles claims friendship of some sort. But as Starways was Liverpool's National Airline, so to speak, we really did carry those four boys a great deal, over the years, in fact years before they were well-known and after they became famous.

Working as we did with little time off and most of us being in our mid-twenties, we girls did not frequent teenage clubs such as the Cavern. So I never saw the Beatles perform live.

All we saw amongst our passengers were four long-haired, leather-jacketed, humorous, cheeky young men. Paul, who was the friendliest and most outgoing of the four, did not like flying one bit. He would always sit at the rear of the aircraft next to whichever stewardess was on board.

On take-off he would keep me entertained by reading fan letters out of magazines – 'Eileen of Chingford,' he quoted, 'it's so wonderful to know the Beatles smoke and drink, it's so good to know they are human!' 'I'm human!' quipped Paul in a Bugs Bunny voice.

'What are you doing tonight, Eileen?' And so the Liverpool humour would never stop and I would laugh for most of the flight as we served the passengers. The only time I ever got nervous when they were on board was when our Chairman and Owner, Mr F H Wilson, was also travelling.

Mr Wilson always sat halfway along the cabin

and when Paul & Co were on board, Paul would always be on the back seat. On take-off, I would say with great seriousness that Mr Wilson was on board but to no avail. After the seatbelt sign was turned off Paul would lift his hands up like a rabbit and almost hop the few seats and stop behind Mr Wilson, saying in a Bugs Bunny voice, 'Eh, hello Mr Wilson.'

With the roar of our engines and the fact Mr Wilson may have been a little hard of hearing this whole episode went unnoticed by our Boss. I would come behind Paul and plead 'you'll get me into trouble.' But these boys were always so very funny we would arrive wherever we were going harassed but laughing.

One day the Beatles were checking in at Heathrow for our midday flight to Liverpool. In walked Captain Leigh who was crew that day. He looked at the four boys and remarked 'if we had you lot in the RAF you'd get a good haircut.' 'You're only jealous 'cos you're bald,' came the dry reply from John Lennon.

For most of the many months that we carried the Beatles they were unknown outside the city of Liverpool and as entertainers were virtually unknown to the airline staff. We just got used to carrying them as regular passengers. So it was a shock one midday at Heathrow to see screaming girls hanging over all the balconies.

I thought a Hollywood film star had arrived. As the Beatles boarded our aircraft, having arrived back from Hamburg, I didn't really associate them with the girls. The flight was only half full so I spent a little more time on our Dakota listening to Paul's non-stop funny chatter.

At Liverpool airport the aircraft always came to a stop no more than 50 feet from the main terminal arrival building so on opening the door I was surprised to find we were parked quite some distance from the building. Through the door I could hear an enormous amount of noise coming from somewhere. Within seconds, Mr Kent, our Station Manager, boarded to collect the ship's papers.

'Collins,' he said, 'keep those four boys on board (he pointed to Paul, the only one visible). There's thousands of screaming females all over the airport, if those boys get off there'll be a riot.' Totally unaware of their rise to fame and that this day was the start of 'Beatlemania' I laughed and joked with this funny, down-to-earth foursome until a car arrived to whisk them away.

The really amazing thing was how, on later trips, these now-famous boys remained the same. They still kept a brilliant sense of humour. Paul still sat on the back seat and one day he said casually 'do you like our music? Be truthful,' he quipped. Being eight or nine years older than them and having never consciously heard them apart from maybe on the radio, I didn't know what to say.

'Well I'm probably a bit old and your music is more for teenagers,' I said, kindly. 'You mean you don't like it?' 'I honestly haven't heard much.' He howled with laughter at my answer. Embarrassed, I remained silent.

Embarrassed I should be, for having been totally unaware of these four boys who changed musical history. I never asked for an autograph and even now, 40 years later, I can only remember them as delightful boys. George dreamily looking out of the window; John's serious, sometimes moody, stare into space; Ringo's unease – a shyness and detachment from us – and Paul's funny, cheeky, non-stop chatter.

Always these four were polite, respectful, great fun and very, very happy to be on their way home to Liverpool.

One of our hostesses, a very beautiful girl, joined Starways at 19 years old. Gaynor Lansberg grew up and went to school with Paul McCartney so it was fun for them to meet again when Gay was a hostess and Paul our passenger. However, one of their flights turned out to be not so funny at all.

As mentioned, the Liverpool boys always sat on separate window seats whenever possible. Halfway through the flight Gaynor walked down the Dakota gangway and to her horror saw the window by which John Lennon was sitting had opened. He, looking even more horrified, panicked as Gay moved him to a safe seat and proceeded at haste to the cockpit. Hardly able to get the words out, she explained to Captain Feenan what had happened.

His reply, in a lazy, laid-back voice told her: 'it won't open any more and not to worry, we'll be landing soon.' Unconvinced, Gaynor returned to the window and grabbed hold of the handle.

Paul came to see what the fuss was and helped by hanging on to Gay only to be joined by George Harrison who held tightly onto Paul and that is how they landed. The three of them hanging onto the window while John Lennon and Ringo Starr kept as far away as possible. Of course, the Captain was right, the Dakota being an unpressurised aircraft, its windows could open a little but the outside pressure would ensure it stayed that way.

A fun night out in Hamburg. Patsy is in the foreground being cuddled by First Officer Mike Tracy. Sitting directly behind her, beneath the left arm of the conductor of the Oompah band, is fellow Air Hostess Gay Landsberg.

Two weeks later, Gaynor was to see the Beatles again as they returned from the USA. The joyful four boarded Starways for Liverpool in an elated state – why? Well BEA (British European Airways) had presented them with travel airline bags that displayed BEA(TLES) on the side. They couldn't have been more made up and proud of their presents as they sat all the way to Liverpool clutching these special bags.

Incidentally, Gaynor's most embarrassing flight was on her 21st birthday flying from Liverpool to Santander. The Captain's report sheets were being passed from passenger to passenger down the aircraft amid grins, which eventually turned to laughter. Gaynor waited patiently as the report finally reached her hands. There she read in bold capital letters: YOUR HOSTESS, HOUMINI BRACE YOUR GIRDLE IS 21 TODAY! Gaynor's beautiful face turned decidedly pink as she braced herself to give them hell in the cockpit but she was stopped from trying to make her way forward by passengers bearing gifts.

She stood transfixed as chocolates and a multitude of other gifts, even a bunch of red roses, were placed in her arms. These presents were obviously meant for the passengers' nearest and dearest, but with smiles and generosity they parted with their precious gifts and brought tears to Gaynor's eyes.

FRANKIE HOWERD

A COMEDIAN who was totally opposite to Ken Dodd was Frankie Howerd. He only travelled on my flights four or five times but he was a miserable person to have as a passenger. Always surly, never a smile. He would ask for something in a demanding voice with never a 'please' or 'thank you.'

One flight he complained throughout the trip and it was a great relief to see this sad, unhappy man leave the aircraft when we landed.

DUCHESS OF WESTMINSTER

THE DOWAGER Duchess of Westminster was delightful. She travelled with us so many times I gave up counting. Nearly always she wore a full-length mink coat and sat looking calmly out of the aircraft window. Her voice was always soft and although middle-aged she had an angelic beauty that was timeless, and the persona of an angel. I loved her without knowing her and when she boarded an aircraft it was as if her spirit filled the cabin.

Many times during her flights we had delays and things went wrong. But each incident was met with graciousness so serene and loving one could hardly believe she wasn't heaven-sent.

If her son, the present Duke of Westminster, has the lovely nature of one of the most beautiful human beings I've ever had the good fortune to meet he will also be a good man to know.

JOE BROWN

SINGER, guitarist and all-round entertainer Joe Brown, a likeable Cockney, was many times on our flights. I don't remember him for any particular reason except, again, a generosity of spirit, fun-loving and for making each flight he was on a happy and enriched travelling time.

GREGORY PECK

ONE day at London's Heathrow my heart stopped on board our DC-4 aircraft! Valery Edwards (London's Station Manager) said, as she handed me ship's papers, 'Gregory Peck is on the flight.' I looked at her, speechless. 'Your mouth is open,' she said. 'Gr-Gregory Peck from Hollywood?' I muttered.

'Gregory Peck, a party of four.' she continued. 'We will bring them on first.' Flushed, with my heart beating so loudly I could hear it and holding my shaking hands together I saw him climb the aircraft steps. As he passed into the cabin he gave the most gorgeous smile and humbly asked which seat he should take. I don't know how I managed to walk straight, let alone appear calm and serene as I led him to his seat for he was one of my idols and this all seemed like a dream.

'We've got him on board for a whole hour,' I said to my fellow stewardess. 'He's not my type,' she replied. 'Oh good, I'll serve them then.'

Gregory Peck's wife and the two gentlemen in their party hadn't a smile between them but he was charming and even better looking off-screen and it was a pleasure just to listen to his beautiful voice. I learned that he was going to the Grand National as he owned one of the racehorses which was entered and, sadly they later had to destroy.

At Liverpool Airport I saw him again. Half an hour after he had disembarked from our flight there he stood, talking to American actress Kim Novak who was by the Aer Lingus desk waiting to board an aircraft to Dublin. As I passed they were laughing together and looked absolutely enchanting.

LIVERPOOL FOOTBALL TEAM

I HAVE been a Liverpool FC supporter since 1961 and I can still remember those famous names: Ian St. John, Roger Hunt, Ron Yeats, Ronnie Morran, Bert Slater and manager Bill Shankly.

Whenever they had an away game in those far-off days, Starways would fly them. The crew always had executive seats to the match and very often a meal as well.

Although I was many times the stewardess on the football flights I can only remember two games out of the ordinary. One was when we flew the team to play Real Madrid and the team bus was stoned by angry Spanish supporters. The other was against Southampton. We had flown to Southampton on Friday for a Saturday match.

It wasn't just Liverpool faring badly abroad. Everton made it to the final of the European Fairs Cup in Milan 1962 but sadly, lost. The passengers drowned their sorrows on the return journey having brought their own crates of beer on board. 'Times have changed, but they were happy and helped the girls to wash up, and had a whip-round for the crew,' recalls Patsy. 'The hostesses were my lovely friends, Ursula Larson and Gay Landsberg.'
Photograph courtesy of the Liverpool Post & Echo

That night a note was pushed under my hotel room door. It said a party was in room 201. Thinking I would join them for a drink I went along only to find a certain striker and a goalkeeper alone with a bottle of Scotch – no party. I didn't go into their room or stay long enough at the door to find out more.

Instead I made my way back to my own room and bed. The next morning I saw the two 'party'-goers at breakfast – their hangovers evident to all! Later we all boarded the bus for Southampton's football ground with not a sign of them. They, apparently, were walking to the stadium still hoping to become part of the land of the living.

Liverpool lost to Southampton 2-0 and I felt very miffed about this so I didn't speak to the striker and goalkeeper on our return flight to Liverpool.

THE BLACK AND WHITE MINSTRELS

ALTHOUGH not politically-correct in today's mixed-up world, The Black and White Minstrel Show was the jewel in London's entertainment crown during the 1960s and 70s. The show ran for years at the Victoria Palace Theatre which was booked to capacity night after night.

Occasionally during their long run, the show went on tour taking its three star singers of the show – John Boulter, Dai Francis and Tony Mercer, plus Stan Stennett who was the resident comedian and musician.

Stan Stennett owned and flew his own aircraft and one particular week whilst the Minstrels were playing at Liverpool's Royal Court Theatre, Stan came to Starways for assistance, bringing with him on this day the star tenor John Boulter. He had a small problem with his aircraft. After it was restored to airworthiness and safely housed in a Starways hangar, all the management were rewarded with complimentary tickets for the show.

Many weeks later Starways reciprocated this kindness when John Boulter and his wife Lorna joined us for a charter flight to Lourdes. Leaving four lovely children behind at home in Wimbledon and exhausted from his amazingly successful show, John and his wife joined us at Liverpool airport for the seven-day break.

After an uneventful flight to France our celebrities decided to join the crew at a hotel in the hills called The Val Fleury where they relaxed, rested and became one of us. The weather was perfect that week and our meals were served outside in the beautiful gardens at one long, long family table.

The food cooked by Madame was simple but extremely good and the wine flowed. Maureen Teabay (the second hostess) and I could hardly contain our excitement at having a star in our midst sharing our walks, meals and evenings out.

So while Maureen and I behaved like 'bobby-soxers' our pilots were unimpressed and indifferent as usual. Two days into our week, our pilot (Captain) called us both to his room. Pacing up and down he began to speak as Maureen and I just stood there. 'These people who have joined us are here for a break,' he announced sternly, 'and the last thing he and his wife want are giggling girls hanging around. His audience is in London. He doesn't need another one in Lourdes.'

We left very subdued after this talk and tried to keep out of the way of everyone. But John and Lorna were so friendly and charming, they seemed delighted to join us for our meals and the entertainment we found in the local community.

Our beautiful week was brought to an end by a very unpleasant return flight. Our DC-4 flew into an unforecast and unexpected electrical storm. As we were tossed about like a boat on the high seas, most of the passengers were sick; some were terrified and not one happy face was seen as daylight was turned into darkness, illuminated only by lightning flashes which transformed the sky into a science fiction odyssey. Suddenly there was a tremendous bang and the aircraft seemed to stop as it shuddered from tail to cockpit. The passengers' grey-looking faces peered at us girls as we held our breath which was only released when we realised we hadn't fallen out of the sky.

On arrival at Liverpool we were to find out how lucky we had been. On checking the aircraft Captain Leigh found a large hole in the DC-4's tail – another inch wider and the hole would have gone through the rudder and we would all have been history. As it was, (once the passengers had departed) the crew, plus John and Lorna Boulter, stood on the tarmac looking up at the aircraft tail and marvelling at our good fortune and miraculous escape.

CHAPTER TEN

H M CUSTOMS

THE gentlemen employed by Her Majesty's Customs and Excise at Liverpool Airport were a great bunch – good humoured, kind and very hard-working. They were almost friends and often delayed crews would be invited to join them around a pot of tea in the Customs Officers' rest room.

In the best Liverpool humour they would chat and joke. Often we would split our sides laughing at some of their stories and the natural comedy and ad-lib was often better than listening to the Goon Show. However, there was one way of instantly removing all trace of comedy or humour from these gentlemen and that was to discuss or ask anything in connection with duty-free entitlements for aircrew and cabin crew.

'Duty-free entitlements for aircrew and cabin crew? You are not entitled to anything!' was the standard reply from one and all. Any pleading or explaining fell on deaf ears.

One day we even had a proper meeting with the Custom officers suggesting that it would not only be reasonable but wise to let us have some – any – sort of allowance.

But the answer: 'you are not legally entitled to anything' prevailed. Another time I had gone along on behalf of all the stewardesses – full of hope and goodwill, to tell them about the Customs at Stansted Airport. They apparently had a book for all regular crews flying in and out of the airport.

Crew members were allowed one bottle of spirits, monthly, plus one bottle of wine and 200 cigarettes and they would sign the book for these. This system kept the crew happy, petty smuggling was unheard of and would cost the guilty their jobs. Looking at the officers' faces as I finished my story I expected a chorus of 'what a good idea', only to be met with stony silence. 'Not a good idea?' I ventured half-heartedly. 'We are only doing our job,' they said.

Undaunted, we tried another channel and three of us went to see our General Manager for help. In our hands was a written request for him to approach the Customs. We stood there for more time than we could spare from our precious little free time as he signed letters, answered phone-calls, called in his secretary half-a-dozen times and was also in the middle of changing our scheduled flight programme.

He looked at the three of us as he picked up the telephone for what seemed like the hundredth time. 'Hang on a moment, Jim,' he said, putting his hand over the receiver and glancing at our brief letter. 'Quite right!' 'You mean, Sir?' we asked. 'I mean they are only doing their job, it would seem,' adding 'against all odds! You girls must realise if Custom Officers say you are not entitled to anything – that is your answer.'

Before we continue, it must be said how much we admired the Customs. They were of high integrity, steadfast, sometimes ruthless but always working 'against all odds'. I'm personally glad they are there nowadays to stop horrendous drug dealers, terrorists and wicked smugglers of any kind! But in 1960 – a bottle of Scotch? Isn't there a happy medium somewhere?

A CAUTIONARY TALE

HELEN Jones (not her real name) had yet to reach her 20th birthday; she was a seasonal hostess, hard-working but immature. Her immaturity appeared in her continual bucking of the system – any system. She arrived late for flights with gay abandon and after a third time was told the next would cost her her job.

Undaunted, she started a personal vendetta against Liverpool's Customs Officers. On one foreign flight with Helen I was busy filling out the Bond Bar forms in preparation for landing when she dipped into the Bar trunk and quite openly took 200 cigarettes. Putting the money into my hand she then turned, unzipped her flight bag, put them on top and zipped it up again. 'You can't go off with those,' I stammered. She smiled, 'I'll go off with what I like.'

'They'll throw the book at you,' I went on. 'You could lose your job.' 'That's a chance I'll have to take,' she answered, brightly. 'Well, I wouldn't risk my job for the whole bar,' I added.

When the passengers had disembarked we proceeded to Customs. Our flight deck crew were a few yards ahead as Helen and I made our way towards an officer. 'Have you anything to declare?' he looked at me. 'A packet of cigarettes.' 'Full?' he enquired. 'Yes.' 'Any more?' Only two cigarettes in another packet.' 'No spirits?' 'No.'

He chalked my bag with a nod and turned to Helen. 'One packet of cigarettes,' she said defiantly before he spoke. 'Anything else?' 'No,' she replied. 'Ok,' he muttered, chalking her bag. We turned to go and my legs felt like jelly sticks as we walked into the main terminal. 'See!' Her cheeky face smiled at me. 'It was one packet but it contained 200 not 20.' 'Well, I admire your guts,' said I.

Helen's fateful flight was a repetition of my first flight with her. She had been getting away with the same trick for weeks and here we were, me standing as the Customs Officer went through my flight bag. He turned to Helen who blatantly said she had one packet. 'How many cigarettes in one packet?' 'It's full,' she answered. 'One packet contains 20 cigarettes, how many have you?' he continued. Oh God, I thought, he knows. 'One packet,' said Helen defiantly.

'For the last time,' he continued, 'how many

cigarettes have you, Miss?' I looked at her and my look screamed, 'tell the truth, he's giving you a chance and you'll only have to pay the duty.' But Helen feared nothing. 'I've told you three times,' she said, with a cheeky reply, 'one packet!' He slowly unzipped her bag, a look of disgust on his face. Helen hadn't even made an attempt to hide the 200 cigarettes that burst forth from her bag.

I was sent on my way by the Customs Officer, the management was called and the last we saw of Helen was her being escorted into the Chief Customs Officer's office. We never saw her again! This time, her luck had run out – she was sacked.

We girls, I will admit, had all sorts of ploys for getting an extra 20 ciggies off the aircraft. We would meet after flights in the upstairs bar and this topic always came up. One suggested three cigarettes in the bottom of your handbag; five in a packet and two in the holdall would make an extra ten ciggies per trip but the loose ones were always broken which stopped that ploy.

A packet under your hat became a favourite. We hated our hats so it was an added bonus that by wearing them we also pleased Betty who continually told us to put our hats on. She, of course, had no idea why all of a sudden they were worn by each and every one of us.

Another girl suggested a packet under each arm! 'That will be noticed!' came our many replies. 'I've done it often' she added and holding a packet of cigarettes she demonstrated as she put her hand inside her blouse and pushed the packet down inside her bra and directly under her arm. 'See there? Completely secure,' she smiled. 'I mean, we don't go into Customs waving our arms madly about so unless you do, they won't show.'

Just a few days later I tried that trick. As we landed, the other hostie and I secured a packet of cigarettes under each arm, they didn't feel particularly comfortable and the corners of the packets scratched our arms as we moved them.

'Just think,' said my fellow smuggler, 'if we have a packet under our hat and one in our bag, plus two under our arms that's 80 ciggies per trip.' 'You're right,' I replied, 'it's worth a bit of discomfort.' In the Customs Hall we stood in line as our bags were checked. The bar box had also been taken off the aircraft where it was normally checked.

Freddie Ferguson, a friendly Customs Officer, was doing the honours but seemed to be having trouble with the lock. He looked up at me and asked, 'are these the right keys?' Having given them to him a moment before, I nodded. 'Well the damn thing won't open, come round here and see if you have better luck.' Forgetting about my underarm cigarettes I turned and bent over the lock only to find it opened with ease at my first attempt and as it did, two hands came from behind and I felt a gentle tickle under each arm.

'Good girl!' he smiled. I looked aghast, knowing full well he had felt the cigarette packets. 'Oh God', I stared at him again and turned scarlet. I waited for him to pounce and as the moments passed I couldn't take my terrified eyes away from his face. His eyes moved from mine to the now open lock. 'Well, open the box,' he grinned, 'have you got your checklist?'

He held out his hand. After checking all was correct Freddie slammed the lid down. 'Well,' he said, looking directly at me, 'let's hope this doesn't happen again.' 'Oh, it won't,' I replied shakily. 'I'll get Mr Kent to replace the padlocks.' 'Right,' he said, 'off you go and don't let it happen again – ever.' I never did put another packet of cigarettes under my arms again.

Most of our Captains, to my knowledge, didn't smuggle, but one who was rather partial to the odd bottle and extra ciggies was the Captain of a Viscount plane who had a short-term contract with the company. Most of the flights I did with him took-off and landed in Manchester. Bill wasn't greedy, mind you, he was happy to put half a bottle under his seat or in his briefcase and if searched he would declare the liquid and pay duty.

Ursula and I were on the last Majorca flight of the season with Bill and to celebrate we each bought a full bottle of spirit and 200 cigarettes. During the return flight the five crew's bottles and cigarettes were duly stowed behind a large, oblong-shaped panel that led from the cockpit into the cabin.

This panel of silver metal was perforated with large round holes, big enough to see through. So to make sure our bottles remained undetected, the

First Officer had covered everything with black carbon paper before screwing back the panel.

We landed in Liverpool and bade farewell to our merry load of holidaymakers. We were just about to disembark ourselves when we noticed six or seven burly men in polo-necked sweaters standing at the bottom of the steps with what looked like axes in their hands.

If this had been the era of hijacking I would have been terrified at what was my first sight of a rummage squad, having only seen Customs Officers in uniform up until then.

As it was, I stood bewildered. 'Rummage Squad,' said the first man to reach the top step. 'Can you inform your Captain?' Still not quite sure who they were I walked up to the cockpit and told Bill. Completely poker-faced, Bill came into the cabin. 'Do you fellows want us to stay on board?' he queried. 'No,' said the leader, 'you clear in the usual way but we would appreciate you not leaving the terminal building for half an hour.'

'No chance of that for at least an hour,' quipped Bill, 'I've a load of paperwork to do and then a cold beer is the order of the day. I was going to put the ground power off but it looks like you fellas will need more light.'

And with that the cockpit, cabin galley and toilets became ablaze with light. My heart sank, we've had it, I thought, as the five of us made our way across the tarmac to the Customs Hall. We had each bought a large gallon casket of wine in Palma for about 10/- (50p) which we declared and paid a small amount of duty on. Then we made our way to the Starways Office and moved away from any 'office ears.'

Patsy on a night flight to Palma in August, 1962. 'I was so worried the photo was taken without my hat on. A mortal sin!'

We then confronted our Captain. 'Bill, what happens if they find our stuff? 'I'm hoping they won't,' he said seriously, 'that's why I gave them plenty of light as the carbon may be more noticeable by torchlight if the aircraft was left in darkness. But with plenty of light there is every chance they won't bother with the exposed panel as they can see in without removing anything.' We all heaved a sigh of relief.

'Anyway, Bill continued, 'if they do find any-thing there's no proof it's ours. The bottles could have been there for weeks.' 'But,' Ursula turned grey as she began to speak, 'I, I've put our names on the bottles.' We stared at her in stony silence. 'You did what!' said Bill in a very angry voice. 'Only our first names, I didn't want to get them mixed up.'

'Are you out of your mind?' Bill replied quietly, yet coldly contemptuous. 'Sorry,' Ursula's eyes gave us all a forlorn look. 'Well, that is it,' continued our Captain. 'There's no way we are going to pass off bottles with Bill, Van, Patsy and Ursula on them as someone else's. You had all better stay in the airport until – by the grace of God – we get cleared to go home.'

It was a very long, long wait. When, with great relief, we finally left the airport it was in the luxury of a taxi. Van suggested we split the fare. He was by now quite inebriated and during the ride to Mossley Hill, where Ursula and I would get out, he suggested he'd show us a wonderful way to make scrambled eggs.

His wife made them, he said, from two pints of milk and six eggs. 'That's impossible.' said I, six eggs won't set in two pints of milk.' Van insisted they would as his wife always made them that way. So Van left the taxi with us and no sooner were we in the house than he filled a saucepan with milk and cracked six eggs into it. Half an hour later we gave Van our remaining half-dozen eggs and he continued to stir the now curdled mixture.

An hour later the mixture looked about the same and it definitely wasn't scrambled eggs. So we finally put Van into another taxi, put the eggs and milk out for whatever animal took a fancy to it and settled for Cola and Marmite sandwiches.

CHAPTER ELEVEN

SORT-OF DISASTERS

CAPTAIN Hammond, Flight Officer Van de Lan and me flew to Cork a week after Starways' inaugural flight there. Starways had been fighting for a scheduled service to Ireland for months and had been awarded one to Cork against all odds and BEA's opposition.

So here we were after landing on the second flight. As I followed Don and Van across the tarmac they were halted by the Station Manager, a fussy, busy little man. 'Oh, Captain Hammond,' he exclaimed in a woeful, singing voice. 'Oh God, Captain Hammond, why in heaven above's name weren't you here last week?'

Don looked behind at me, than at Van and lifted his shoulders in a shrug. 'Bless our souls, Captain Hammond, if only you'd been here de whole dey would have been a blessing instead of a disaster. Oh deary, deary me.' (He was now shaking his head).

'What are you talking about?' said Don in a soft, calm voice. The poor man didn't hear. 'I wanted the ground to open,' he continued, gesturing to the tarmac with both hands, 'and swallow me up.'

Looking harassed and even more woeful, he continued, 'but it didn't, and I had to face dem all and just die while I was still alive! Dere it was,' he raised both his hands dramatically towards the runway, 'de Starways lovely plane landing and here I was with de Mayor and all de important people of Cork and over dere was a big band, as big as an orchestra it was, on de tarmac playing and waiting for de very big moment when de passengers and crew would put dere feet on de soil of Ireland.

'So we waited. De passengers came down de steps all smiling at de lovely welcome we had waiting for dem. And then it happened!' He put his hand to his head, obviously still distressed. We waited with bated breath. 'What happened?' asked Don.

'De Mayor.' The poor man who now looked agonised went on: 'he went forward to greet de crew and dere, oh God I can hardly move me mouth to say it, dere was de Flight Officer with not a uniform on him and behind him came Captain Leigh in a dirty shirt with de sleeves rolled up. Sure, I nearly died and me heart stopped beating. De hostess was de only one who looked like she belonged to Starways. Captain Leigh didn't notice it all but the shame, the shame was with me. I looked at de Mayor's face. Oh Lord, I'll never live it down.' He was now almost in tears.

'Captain Hammond,' he continued, as we started walking and he fell into step beside us, 'you are such a smart man yourself, sure. You look lovely now. I only wish to God it was last week and de Mayor had seen de lovely look of yer.'

We were all trying to suppress our smiles at his serious woe but we couldn't help but feel sorry for the poor man. To him it had been a most special occasion and he had organised the Band and the Mayor's presence with some difficulty. What he hadn't thought of was to inform Liverpool of the fanfare that would greet the first Cork flight so it had all gone horribly wrong.

THE CONGO

DURING the Belgian Congo uprising, Starways had a 12-month contract to fly for the United Nations. One aircraft, DC-4 G-APIN, was painted in UN colours and Starways' crews would operate the aircraft carrying freight.

This particular day in late summer 1961, Captain Bryan Monkton, Flight Officer Carl Ilgis, Malcolm Ebbitt our Chief Engineer and Colin Taberner, another engineer, had just landed at Kamina which was a forward operating base in the Congo for the UN.

Both engineers had disembarked leaving the pilots on board when a French Fouga jet flown by a mercenary and operating on behalf of the President of the breakaway state of Katanga, circled the airport. It then made a run-in and began machine-gunning the tarmac making our strolling engineers run for their lives. The pilots were still on board when the jet made a second run-in, this time firing a rocket directly into the Starways DC-4. The aircraft exploded and caught fire.

Flight Officer Carl Ilgis was very badly wounded, most of his body being hit by shrapnel. With the aircraft now on fire and Carl lying bleeding in the fuselage, Captain Monkton dragged his injured First Officer to the front crew open door and without steps to help them they both dropped 15 feet to the ground. As he landed, Bryan Monkton broke an ankle but they both escaped with their lives.

Starways ultimately terminated the United Nations contract after its aircraft was destroyed. We were, after all, a civilian airline.

Kindu Airport in the Congo was patrolled for the United Nations by troops from Malaya. Wisely, these troops never left the perimeter of the airport and never ventured further. Two Italian Airforce Transport Aircraft flew in one day in November 1961 and for reasons that made no sense at all, the 13 crew members decided to leave the safety of the airport and proceed into Kindu Town.

They strolled about dressed in military camouflage uniforms and were taken by the local residents to be the much despised Belgian paratroopers who had occupied the Congo prior to the Belgian withdrawal. A crowd of locals attacked them with machetes and they were all slaughtered on the spot.

Reports came back that dismembered parts of the Italians had been displayed and sold at the local meat market. From that day on, no other crews left the safety of the airfield. For our Starways' crews the Congo was a very harrowing and fraught operation.

After the turmoil of the Belgian withdrawal, intense tribal warfare broke out with often the primary victims being the few educated Congolese remaining – doctors, teachers, air traffic controllers, radio maintenance personnel.

As a result, there were no navigational aids and three- to four-hour trips had to be made across territory where the maps, if any, had been compiled in the 1890s. As a result, on arrival the aircraft carrying UN supplies often had to carry out a square search of the area to locate an airport.

On arrival, with no air traffic control available, the only means of identifying friend or foe was to make a low pass down the runway to see if the troops were wearing blue helmets indicating that a safe landing could be made. If the crew had got it wrong, shooting would start as they arrived over the airfield boundary.

And after all that, Starways never did get a United Nations Medal!

THE DUBLIN CRASH

A STARWAYS DC-4 aircraft with a full load of 69 passengers and four crew made a wheels-up landing in a grass field outside Dublin Airport perimeter on September 19th, 1961. The aircraft continued sliding through the soft earth to the end of the field, through a fence and onto a main road.

The impact appeared to be so slight and the night so dark that many of the passengers didn't realise they had not landed at the airport and on the runway. The two stewardesses on board were Fay Arista and Barbara Wilkinson. Hardly knowing what had happened themselves, they calmly opened the aircraft cabin doors and the passengers stepped out onto the road and boarded a public service bus which had conveniently come ambling along.

The damaged Starways DC-4 which slid off the runway at Collinstown Airport, Dublin, in September 1961.

This could only have happened in Ireland. There were no injuries to the passengers or crew. Later that night to clear this main Dublin road the aircraft had to be pulled back into the field by a tractor.

A number of claims were subsequently received

by the Starways Company insurers for post-traumatic stress from passengers including a heavy consumption of Irish whiskey for medical reasons only. An investigation attributed the accident to incorrect management of the fuel system by the flight crew, resulting in a partial loss of power and control.

CHAPTER TWELVE

END OF AN ERA

WHEN it was revealed to the pilots, hostesses, and ground staff in 1963 that Starways was to merge with British Eagle, a London-based airline, a gloom cloud descended on our staff. This news sent most of us into a state of apprehension as we were unsure we would still have a job after the Eagles takeover.

By now I had climbed to the exotic height of Chief Stewardess (Betty having left to get married) and really loved my job. We were, of course, all assured our jobs were safe, but still there was a sense of sadness around us as the all-important figure of Mr Bamberg, Eagle's Chairman and his entourage flew between London and Liverpool making the final arrangements.

During Starways' final week of operations insecurity set in, as everything seemed dreamlike and fuzzy as we went about our busy working days. Hour by hour, changes were being made to our scheduled programmes and many new and unknown faces appeared.

Starways staff found it hard to see a familiar face; we spoke in whispers, which was all part of our insecurity. But, whatever happened, we innately

Patsy with the British Eagle hat on. 'We felt silly at the time,' she says.

knew things would never be the same again. And no matter what happened to us it was now a forgone conclusion that Liverpool would lose its own airline, and that at best we would all become part of a London-based enterprise.

So that last week took on a distinct feeling of mourning. Outward signs of change to us were our uniforms. Our BOAC-type navy-blue suit and air force hat was replaced by a maroon box jacket with a bowler-type hat with a peak. And so the last week was to pass and takeover day dawned on December 31st, 1963. The following morning I was put on a flight to Innsbruck with British Eagle's chief steward-ess, a very cheerful and likeable girl. As the flight was empty from Liverpool to London we had an hour to get to know each other. Then, at Heathrow it was a shock for me to find our complement of passengers for Innsbruck was three. Having been used to the aircraft always being full it was embarrassing to hear my colleague address them over the PA system as Ladies and Gentlemen when all three were men.

I mentioned how astonished I was to be on a flight to Austria with only three passengers. 'Oh you'll get used to it,' she replied. 'Would it not be better to speak to just three passengers personally rather than over the PA system?'

No, I was informed, rules were rules. Also, 36 hot meals had been placed on board, enough for half an aircraft load but with only three passengers and four crew to eat, to me this was another ridiculous extravagance. To my dismay, all untouched meals were put into a rubbish bin before our arrival at Innsbruck.

The return flight was even worse – there was only one passenger for Heathrow but we still had the same impersonal announcements and another complement of 36 meals. Querying this waste of food with my colleague I asked if, this time, the meals could be left on board until we reached Liverpool. 'I'm afraid that is not allowed,' she said. 'All untouched food must be binned before landing.'

'But it's good food,' I pleaded, adding that I'd be happy to take a meal or two home and I knew that the ground staff at Speke would be delighted to have some. But my words were in vain. Rules were rules and I watched with sadness as untouched food was discarded by the cartload.

Seeing my stricken face my colleague gave my shoulder a reassuring squeeze, saying: 'You've just got to start thinking big now you're no longer with a small-time outfit.'

Having witnessed people starving around the world I still found food destruction hard to come to terms with. The following week of flying brought more questions from me. 'How can a company operate like this?' I questioned one girl.

'Don't worry about silly things like that,' came the reply, 'the Chairman doesn't, he's just written off £3 million.' I turned and looked at her. 'Written off? Do you mean he's lost the money?' 'Oh no,' she smiled, 'not lost, he's just too rich to bother about it.' I shook my head and sat down and wrote my letter of resignation.

For me it was the change between a way of life and a job – and time to move on. Or maybe some innate sense of business was disturbed by Eagle's wasteful operating practices. The company was to last longer than I envisaged but it finally went into bankruptcy in 1968.

And so the people of Liverpool lost their very own airline. Starways, during its 16-year lifetime from 1948 to 1963 had made a profit, provided many jobs for Liverpudlians, and instilled a sense of loyalty which would be almost impossible to find today.

Most of all, it was an avenue for the warmth, humour and fun which makes Liverpool's people so special. Thankfully all this still lives on today within the city. For no matter who or what comes and goes, Starways was only an outward expression of the very essence and spirit of Liverpool's wonderful people!

EPILOGUE

STARWAYS disappeared from the aviation world 50 years ago. I am still in touch with some of the girls. Sadly, all the pilots and management (bar one) have left the circuit of life. Bernie Mackenzie, our most helpful engineer, is still in touch and still smiling.

But there was one who remained in my life for 50 adventurous years, who I'll come to in a moment. I haven't mentioned boyfriends but I had three during my flying years. The first was Mark Royes, a Starways First Officer.

Born in Jamaica, Mark's father was English and his mum Jamaican. We went out for about a year and I was very sad and confused when Mark said he could not go on seeing me.

Patsy with First Officer Mark Royes, her boyfriend during her first year flying.

I asked him why. 'Captain Leigh is watching me because I'm with you.'

'That is utterly ridiculous,' I answered. 'I hardly know the man, he knows my brother-in-law as they were in the RAF together.' 'Whatever,' replied Mark, and we parted.

My second boyfriend was a passenger – an efficiency expert who flew Starways every Monday to a job in Scotland and home to Liverpool every Friday evening, so we only went out at weekends, if I wasn't flying.

One Friday after a night out Paul and I were having a cuddle in his car outside my flat – suddenly I saw Captain Leigh walk by. I was stunned. I looked at my watch to see if it was past midnight. Aware I was on an early morning flight abroad. I told Paul I had better go and kissed him good night. I had only been in my flat a couple of minutes when there came a loud rap, rap at my front door. On opening the door I came face to face with Captain Leigh.

Thinking some terrible emergency had taken place, I just stared at him. He broke the silence, saying: 'Miss Collins, are you aware you are flying at 7am tomorrow and reporting for duty at 6am?' Still shocked, I stammered 'yes Sir.' 'Well if your social life continues to be more important than your career your job will not last very long, I suggest you get some sleep, good night.' He turned and left.

I closed the door and went to bed a nervous wreck. In those days it never occurred to me to question why he was outside my flat at midnight – you just didn't question authority!

Don Wolff was someone I had known since I was 18 years old. He was a pilot with Scottish Airlines.

My brother-in-law, Laird Kennedy, introduced us and I lost my heart there and then but Don was a loner. In those days he would go out to Iraq, flying small aircraft for the oil industry.

For six years we wrote to each other weekly. I saw Don during all his annual leave. When I started flying he would spend most of his leave in Liverpool staying at the Exchange Hotel. In 1963, Don sent me a BEA (British European Airways) ticket and asked me to join him for a week's holiday in Majorca.

I took my annual week's leave and flew to Spain. Don had booked two rooms in a lovely hotel and he told me he had planned a surprise for the second day of our holiday. At dinner that evening he mentioned it was an important day for us tomorrow; we would be visiting some caves, but was quite mysterious about his plans. Excited, the next morning I hurriedly showered, ready to join Don for breakfast and our trip, only to find he wasn't in the dining room.

I rang Don's room but there was no reply. The reception then informed me he had left early that morning. Puzzled as to what had happened I spent the day feeling lost, mystified and hurt.

That evening he returned and was withdrawn and sad. Don's excuse for leaving without me was that I had come down too late to join him, which I knew was untrue. But he was upset about something and for the next two days we were polite to each other but our holiday was obviously ruined. I then decided to return home and Don stayed on in Majorca.

On his return he phoned me and asked me who 'K' was? I did not know. 'Why do you ask me?' I queried. 'It doesn't matter now,' was his reply.

A Starways Viscount

Don never missed sending a Christmas card and letter to my family. Some 20 years after I had known him at Starways, he wrote to say he was passing through our town and would I join him for coffee. During coffee he mentioned Majorca and told me that on the morning of our cave visit, a card had arrived for me by courier. Reception had handed it to Don. It read: 'Have no fear. "K" is here guarding you.'

Don had intended to propose that day and still had the ring. 'Why didn't you show me that card?' I asked. I thought you had someone in your life,' he answered.

He was wrong, but 'K' was none other than Starways pilot Captain George Keith Leigh – who had evidently been determined to win me for himself and eventually got his way!

When I returned home from my coffee with Don I gave my husband some stick. 'How could you do that – send a card to someone on holiday with a boyfriend?' I admonished. 'Anyway, how did you know where I was?' 'Your sister told me,' he replied. 'Anyway, your silly boyfriend should have put the card in the bin. Faint heart never won fair maiden.' 'Oh really?' I huffed. I had always thought that my loss of boyfriends those past four years was my fault!

I recall the night that Captain Leigh finally got his chance to woo me. After flights I would often visit my sister Barbara and her new baby Sarah. One evening I found my sister in tears and extremely distressed. She kept repeating, 'I hate him.' 'Hate who?' I asked. 'George Leigh,' came the reply. 'Every night he comes here and takes Laird out for a drink and I'm left alone with Sarah.'

Ursula arrived amid the tears. 'Right, pull yourself together,' she said to Barbie. 'Go and get changed, you are going out tonight.'

We all had supper and at approximately 8pm, George Leigh arrived. He stood in the open doorway and said, 'let's go for a beer, Jock.' 'One minute,' said Ursula. 'Barbie is coming with you. We will look after Sarah.'

The two men stood open-mouthed, still in the

doorway. Captain Leigh was the first to speak. 'Does it take two of you to look after one small baby?' he asked. Turning to me, he said, 'you can come too.'

Reluctant to leave Ursula, my eyes pleaded with her. 'You go. Good luck,' she quipped.

That was my first date with Captain George Leigh – the man I was to marry and spend 50 adventurous years with.

Captain George Keith Leigh, left, with Starways' Chairman Frank Wilson on the flight deck of a Viscount G-ARIR in February 1961, on the day it was delivered to Starways.
Photograph courtesy of the Liverpool Post & Echo

A pilot stood at the Golden Gates,
His head was bent and low,
He gently asked the man of fate,
Which way he had to go.
'What have you done on Earth' he cried,
'To seek admittance here?',
'I flew a plane for Starways,
For many a long year'.
St Peter opened wide the gate,
He beamed on him as well,
'Step inside and choose a harp,
You've had your share of Hell!'

Frank Carroll
A Starways pilot

Thumbs up from holidaymakers as they prepare to fly with Starways, Liverpool's much-loved airline.

Photograph courtesy of the Liverpool Post & Echo

Starways: When Liverpool Ruled The Skies is available in paperback from all good book stores or can be ordered online from Amazon. It is also available as an e-book.

Bramblewood Publishing is based in Overton-on-Dee, North Wales. You can contact the publishers by email: Bramblewoodpublishing@outlook.com or via the website: www.bramblewoodpublishing.co.uk

14973361R00087

Printed in Poland
by Amazon Fulfillment
Poland Sp. z o.o., Wrocław